Bloom's BioCritiques

Dante Alighieri
Maya Angelou
Jane Austen
The Brontë Sisters
Lord Byron
Geoffrey Chaucer
Anton Chekhov
Joseph Conrad
Stephen Crane
Charles Dickens
Emily Dickinson
William Faulkner
F. Scott Fitzgerald
Robert Frost
Ernest Hemingway
Langston Hughes
Zora Neale Hurston
Stephen King
Arthur Miller
John Milton
Toni Morrison
Edgar Allan Poe
J. D. Salinger
William Shakespeare
John Steinbeck
Henry David Thoreau
Mark Twain
Alice Walker
Walt Whitman
Tennessee Williams

Bloom's BioCritiques

ZORA NEALE HURSTON

Edited and with an introduction by
Harold Bloom
Sterling Professor of the Humanities
Yale University

CHELSEA HOUSE
PUBLISHERS
A Haights Cross Communications Company
Philadelphia

©2003 by Chelsea House Publishers, a subsidiary of
Haights Cross Communications.

A Haights Cross Communications Company

Introduction © 2003 by Harold Bloom.

10 9 8 7 6 5 4 3 2 1

Library of Congress Cataloging-in-Publication Data
Zora Neale Hurston / edited and with an introduction by Harold Bloom.
    p. cm. -- (Bloom's biocritiques)
  ISBN 0-7910-7386-6
  1. Hurston, Zora Neale--Criticism and interpretation. 2. Women and
literature--United States--History--20th century. 3. African Americans
in literature. 4. Folklore in literature. I. Bloom, Harold. II.
Series.
  PS3515.U789Z96 2003
  813'.52--dc21

                                            2002155107

Chelsea House Publishers
1974 Sproul Road, Suite 400
Broomall, PA 19008-0914

http://www.chelseahouse.com

Contributing editor: Amy Sickels

Cover design by Keith Trego

Cover: © CORBIS

Layout by EJB Publishing Services

CONTENTS

User's Guide

These volumes are designed to introduce the reader to the life and work of the world's literary masters. Each volume begins with Harold Bloom's essay "The Work in the Writer" and a volume-specific introduction also written by Professor Bloom. Following these unique introductions is an engaging biography that discusses the major life events and important literary accomplishments of the author under consideration.

Furthermore, each volume includes an original critique that not only traces the themes, symbols, and ideas apparent in the author's works, but strives to put those works into a cultural and historical perspective. In addition to the original critique is a brief selection of significant critical essays previously published on the author and his or her works followed by a concise and informative chronology of the writer's life. Finally, each volume concludes with a bibliography of the writer's works, a list of additional readings, and an index of important themes and ideas.

HAROLD BLOOM

The Work in the Writer

Literary biography found its masterpiece in James Boswell's *Life of Samuel Johnson*. Boswell, when he treated Johnson's writings, implicitly commented upon Johnson as found in his work, even as in the great critic's life. Modern instances of literary biography, such as Richard Ellmann's lives of W. B. Yeats, James Joyce, and Oscar Wilde, essentially follow in Boswell's pattern.

That the writer somehow is in the work, we need not doubt, though with William Shakespeare, writer-of-writers, we almost always need to rely upon pure surmise. The exquisite rancidities of the Problem Plays or Dark Comedies seem to express an extraordinary estrangement of Shakespeare from himself. When we read or attend *Troilus and Cressida* and *Measure for Measure*, we may be startled by particular speeches of Ulysses in the first play, or of Vincentio in the second. These speeches, of Ulysses upon hierarchy or upon time, or of Duke Vincentio upon death, are too strong either for their contexts or for the characters of their speakers. The same phenomenon occurs with Parolles, the military impostor of *All's Well That Ends Well*. Utterly disgraced, he nevertheless affirms: "Simply the thing I am/Shall make me live."

In Shakespeare, more even than in his peers, Dante and Cervantes, meaning always starts itself again through excess or overflow. The strongest of Shakespeare's creatures—Falstaff, Hamlet, Iago, Lear, Cleopatra—have an exuberance that is fiercer than their plays can contain. If Ben Jonson was at all correct in his complaint that "Shakespeare wanted art," it could have been only in a sense that he may not have intended. Where do the personalities of Falstaff or Hamlet touch a limit? What was it in Shakespeare that made the two parts of *Henry IV* and *Hamlet* into "plays unlimited"? Neither Falstaff nor Hamlet will be stopped: their wit, their beautiful, laughing speech, their intensity of being—all these are virtually infinite.

In what ways do Falstaff and Hamlet manifest the writer in the work? Evidently, we can never know, or know enough to answer with any authority. But what would happen if we reversed the question, and asked: How did the work form the writer, Shakespeare?

Of Shakespeare's inwardness, his biography tells us nothing. And yet, to an astonishing extent, Shakespeare created our inwardness. At the least, we can speculate that Shakespeare so lived his life as to conceal the depths of his nature, particularly as he rather prematurely aged. We do not have Shakespeare on Shakespeare, as any good reader of the Sonnets comes to realize: they do not constitute a key that unlocks his heart. No sequence of sonnets could be less confessional or more powerfully detached from the poet's self.

The German poet and universal genius, Goethe, affords a superb contrast to Shakespeare. Of Goethe's life, we know more than everything; I wonder sometimes if we know as much about Napoleon or Freud or any other human being who ever has lived, as we know about Goethe. Everywhere, we can find Goethe in his work, so much so that Goethe seems to crowd the writing out, just as Byron and Oscar Wilde seem to usurp their own literary accomplishments. Goethe, cunning beyond measure, nevertheless invested a rival exuberance in his greatest works that could match his personal charisma. The sublime outrageousness of the Second Part of *Faust*, or of the greater lyric and meditative poems, form a Counter-Sublime to Goethe's own daemonic intensity.

Goethe was fascinated by the daemonic in himself; we can doubt that Shakespeare had any such interests. Evidently, Shakespeare abandoned his acting career just before he composed *Measure for Measure* and *Othello*. I surmise that the egregious interventions by Vincentio and Iago displace the actor's energies into a new kind of mischief-making, a fresh opening to a subtler playwriting-within-the-play.

But what had opened Shakespeare to this new awareness? The answer is the work in the writer, *Hamlet* in Shakespeare. One can go further: it was not so much the play, *Hamlet*, as the character Hamlet, who changed Shakespeare's art forever.

Hamlet's personality is so large and varied that it rivals Goethe's own. Ironically Goethe's Faust, his Hamlet, has no personality at all, and is as colorless as Shakespeare himself seems to have chosen to be. Yet nothing could be more colorful than the Second Part of *Faust*, which is peopled by an astonishing array of monsters, grotesque devils, and classical ghosts.

A contrast between Shakespeare and Goethe demonstrates that in each—but in very different ways—we can better find the work in the person, than we can discover that banal entity, the person in the work. Goethe to many of his contemporaries, seemed to be a mortal god. Shakespeare, so far as we know, seemed an affable, rather ordinary fellow, who aged early and became somewhat withdrawn. Yet Faust, though Mephistopheles battles for his soul, is hardly worth the trouble unless you take him as an idea and not as a person. Hamlet is nearly every-idea-in-one, but he is precisely a personality and a person.

Would Hamlet be so astonishingly persuasive if his father's ghost did not haunt him? Falstaff is more alive than Prince Hal, who says that the devil haunts him in the shape of an old fat man. Three years before composing the final *Hamlet*, Shakespeare invented Falstaff, who then never ceased to haunt his creator. Falstaff and Hamlet may be said to best represent the work in the writer, because their influence upon Shakespeare was prodigious. W.H. Auden accurately observed that Falstaff possesses infinite energy: never tired, never bored, and absolutely both witty and happy until Hal's rejection destroys him. Hamlet too has infinite energy, but in him it is more curse than blessing.

Falstaff and Hamlet can be said to occupy the roles in Shakespeare's invented world that Sancho Panza and Don Quixote possess in Cervantes's. Shakespeare's plays from 1610 on (starting with *Twelfth Night*) are thus analogous to the Second Part of Cervantes's epic novel. Sancho and the Don overtly jostle Cervantes for authorship in the Second Part, even as Cervantes battles against the impostor who has pirated a continuation of his work. As a dramatist, Shakespeare manifests the work in the writer more indirectly. Falstaff's prose genius is revived in the scapegoating of Malvolio by Maria and Sir Toby Belch, while Falstaff's darker insights are developed by Feste's melancholic wit. Hamlet's intellectual resourcefulness, already deadly, becomes poisonous in Iago and in Edmund. Yet we have not crossed into the deeper abysses of the work in the writer in later Shakespeare.

No fictive character, before or since, is Falstaff's equal in self-trust. Sir John, whose delight in himself is contagious, has total confidence both in his self-awareness and in the resources of his language. Hamlet, whose self is as strong, and whose language is as copious, nevertheless distrusts both the self and language. Later Shakespeare is, as it were, much under the influence both of Falstaff and of Hamlet, but they tug him in opposite directions. Shakespeare's own copiousness of language is well-nigh incredible: a vocabulary in excess of twenty-one thousand words, almost eighteen hundred of which he coined himself. And of his word-hoard, nearly half are used only once each, as though the perfect setting for each had been found, and need not be repeated. Love for language and faith in language are Falstaffian attributes. Hamlet will darken both that love and that faith in Shakespeare, and perhaps the Sonnets can best be read as Falstaff and Hamlet counterpointing against one another.

Can we surmise how aware Shakespeare was of Falstaff and Hamlet, once they had played themselves into existence? *Henry IV, Part I* appeared in six quarto editions during Shakespeare's lifetime; *Hamlet* possibly had four. Falstaff and Hamlet were played again and again at the Globe, but Shakespeare knew also that they were being read, and he must have had contact with some of those readers. What would it have been like to discuss Falstaff or Hamlet with one of their early readers (presumably also part of their audience at the Globe), if you were the creator of such demiurges? The question would seem nonsensical to most Shakespeare scholars, but then these days they tend to be either ideologues or moldy figs. How can we recover the uncanniness of Falstaff and of Hamlet, when they now have become so familiar?

A writer's influence upon himself is an unexplored problem in criticism, but such an influence is never free from anxieties. The biocritical problem (which this series attempts to explore) can be divided into two areas, difficult to disengage fully. Accomplished works affect the author's life, and also affect her subsequent writings. It is simpler for me to surmise the effect of *Mrs. Dalloway* and *To the Lighthouse* upon Woolf's late *Between the Acts*, than it is to relate Clarissa Dalloway's suicide and Lily Briscoe's capable endurance in art to the tragic death and complex life of Virginia Woolf.

There are writers whose lives were so vivid that they seem sometimes to obscure the literary achievement: Byron, Wilde, Malraux, Hemingway. But most major Western writers do not live that exuberantly, and the greatest of all, Shakespeare, sometimes appears to have adopted the personal mask of colorlessness. And yet there are heroes of literature who struggled titanically with their own eras— Tolstoy, Milton, Victor Hugo—who nevertheless matter more for their works than their lives.

There are great figures—Emily Dickinson, Wallace Stevens, Willa Cather—who seem to have had so little of the full intensity of life when compared to the vitality of their work, that we might almost speak of the work in the work, rather than even of the work in a person. Emily Brontë might well be the extreme instance of such a visionary, surpassing William Blake in that one regard.

I conclude this general introduction to a series of literary bio-critiques by stating a tentative formula or principle for gauging the many ways in which the work influences the person and her subsequent, later work. Our influence upon ourselves is always related to the Shakespearean invention of self-overhearing, which I have written about in several other contexts. Life, as well as poetry and prose, is overheard rather than simply heard. The writer listens to herself as though she were somebody else, and the will to change begins to operate. The forces that live in us include the prior work we have done, and the dreams and waking visions that evade our dismissals.

HAROLD BLOOM

Introduction

Hurston was a vitalist, enormously alive. Sometimes I find myself thinking of her as a Shakespearean character, so much does she now belong to American literary legend. Of all major African-American writers, she appears to have possessed the most personal verve, a life-force wonderfully embodied in *Their Eyes Were Watching God* (surely one of the great titles).

Flamboyant writers—Lord Byron, Oscar Wilde, Hemingway—manifest a curious relationship of the work to the life, one that breaks down the wavering demarcation between art and reality. Hurston—novelist, anthropologist, folklorist—had a fierce dislike of racial politics, black *and* white, and loathed any attempt to subsume her individuality under any category whatsoever.

We all of us pay high prices for our freedom from cant, social dogma, and societal morality. Hurston, passionate and driven by a *daemon*, plunged into a terrible final decade, in which she alienated most of her friends, admirers, readers. She *opposed* desegregation, arguing that it would degrade black education. Rejected by the publishing world and by foundations, she died in a welfare home, and was buried in an unmarked grave. Her mourners all have been retrospective.

Ralph Ellison, a great writer and a warm acquaintance, once at dinner together told me he could not understand my admiration for *Their Eyes Were Watching God*, a novel he found alternately overwritten and underwritten. I recall replying that the book's vitalism disarmed me: if the style was uneven, the abundant surge of outrageous will to live in the heroine Janie had a cosmic urgency, a persuasiveness I could not resist. Hurston is that rare author who mothered herself into existence. She has a gusto that reminds me of Chaucer's the Wife of Bath and Shakespeare's Sir John Falstaff. It was probably inevitable that she would immerse herself in the destructive element, but she achieved one undying book, heroic and poignant.

NORMA JEAN LUTZ

Biography of Zora Neale Hurston

THE FIRST BOOK

For many citizens in the United States, 1933 was a year of unprecedented hardships. The stock market crash of October 29, 1929 (referred to as "Black Tuesday"), had left the country reeling and plunged it into the Great Depression. During the next few years, ten thousand banks failed, resulting in the loss of over $2 billion in deposits. More than thirteen million citizens were out of work. In every major city, people stood for hours in long lines, seeking employment or waiting for handouts from the many soup kitchens.

While times were difficult for everyone, they were especially difficult for the black population, and more difficult still for black artists and writers who, already at the lower end of the economic stratum in times of prosperity, now found day-to-day subsistence almost impossible.

One such writer was Zora Neale Hurston, a published author who, after many years of living in New York, had returned to her childhood home of Eatonville, Florida to compile into one manuscript the materials she'd gathered through her work as an anthropologist. Glad to be back, she wrote to friends, "The air is sweet, literally sweet." (Hemenway, 162)

When she completed the manuscript, entitled *Mules and Men*, she set it aside until she could find a publisher for it and turned her attention

3

to the production of her musical *Sun to Sun*. She contacted the English department of Rollins College in nearby Winter Park, whose professors agreed to subsidize two presentations of the revue. While the work was fun and fulfilling, it paid little, and Hurston was nearly desperate for funds.

She turned her pen to writing short stories in hopes of generating income. When she presented one of her stories, "The Gilded Six-Bits," to Robert Wunsch of the English department at Rollins, he read it to his class, then sent the story off to *Story Magazine*, where it was accepted for publication in the August 1933 issue.

Story Magazine was so respected at this time that many editors at New York publishing houses sought promising new writers in its pages. Four such editors contacted Hurston, asking for full-length works, but she answered only one—Bertram Lippincott of the J.B. Lippincott Publishing Company. She assured him she had a novel underway and would send it to him soon.

While Hurston may have had a plot in mind, she had no actual work done on her novel. In keeping with her spirit of fierce determination, she set about to write one. She moved to the town of Sanford, Florida, where she was "not so much at home as at Eatonville, and could concentrate more" (Hurston, 153), and rented a small house for $1.50 a week. The first two weeks' rent took all of her money, so she turned to a kind cousin who lived in Sanford, who gave Hurston fifty cents of her $3.50 a week income to purchase needed groceries.

Sitting at a rickety card table, Hurston wrote day after day for three months. By September 4, she could tell Lippincott that the manuscript was nearly ready. While she was excited that her novel was so close to submission, she still needed to have the manuscript typed, and asked the secretary to the town's municipal judge to read the work. The secretary agreed to type the manuscript and wait for payment, confident that if Lippincott did not purchase the novel, someone else would.

By October 3, 1933, the manuscript was ready to mail, and now Hurston needed $1.83 to purchase the postage. This time she turned to Mrs. John Leonardi of Sanford, wife of the County Prosecutor and a lawyer in her own right. Mrs. Leonardi did not have the money, but she was the treasurer for the local Daughter of the Elks organization, and borrowed two dollars from their treasury to loan to Hurston.

By this time, Hurston owed eighteen dollars in back rent, and her landlady was growing impatient. Hurston planned to pay the rent from the $25 she would earn performing with her concert group for the Seminole County Chamber of Commerce, but on the morning of October 16, she was evicted from the little house. She took her belongings to her uncle's house and hurried on to the concert.

Following the concert, all cast members received both payment and certificates good at any store in town. Hurston went to the nearest shoe store to replace her worn-out shoes; while trying on new shoes, she remembered the telegram in her pocket that had been handed to her earlier in the day. She tore it open to find an offer from Bertram Lippincott to purchase her novel *Jonah's Gourd Vine*, with an advance of $200—more money than she'd seen in a very long time. She raced from the shoe store to the Western Union office, wearing one new shoe and one old shoe, to wire her acceptance of the offer.

Though awards and other contracts would come her way throughout her long and illustrious writing career, no event would ever be as special to Hurston as the moment when she received that notice of the acceptance of her first book.

EATONVILLE, FLORIDA

On January 1, 1863, the institution of slavery officially ended in the United States when President Abraham Lincoln issued the Emancipation Proclamation. As word spread throughout the South, many slaves simply walked away from the plantations. Others joined the Union forces. Thousands were displaced and left homeless, without food, shelter, or clothing.

In the years following the war, thanks to Reconstruction and the outreach programs of black churches, freed slaves had unprecedented opportunities for advancement. Many black men were voted into state and local offices during Reconstruction—South Carolina's legislature following the Civil War was made up of eighty-seven blacks and forty whites. The state would later have black lieutenant governors in two consecutive terms.

This trend came to a sudden halt in 1876, when Rutherford B. Hayes came into office and ordered all Union troops (and all other restrictions with regard to Reconstruction) to be withdrawn from the South. A few years later, in 1883, the Supreme Court outlawed the Civil Rights Act of 1875, and "Jim Crow" laws came into existence that banned blacks from public places such as hotels, restaurants, theaters, and trains. The Southern black population saw political and social gains quickly slipping away until, by the end of the century, their way of life became little better than what they'd known in the days of slavery. Thousands became sharecroppers, farming land that belonged to white landowners and being allowed to keep only a small portion of the profits.

One such sharecropper was John Hurston from Macon County, Alabama. He worked a cotton plantation near Notasulga, an area other blacks considered "over the creek"—in other words, on the wrong side of the tracks. Over-the-creek blacks occupied the lowest social level.

Somehow John Hurston had learned to read and write, and he possessed an inner longing to better himself. When he was nearly twenty, he started attending the Macedonia Baptist Church—located on the *right* side of the creek—every Sunday morning. In the choir there, he noticed pretty Lucy Potts, the fourteen-year-old daughter of landowner Richard Potts. He stared at her all through the services, and was soon not only eyeing her, but slipping her notes in the pages of the hymnbook. Lucy eventually decided to marry him.

Landowners from the right side of the creek normally had nothing to do with the sharecroppers from the wrong side of the creek, finding little respect for those who had "no more pride than to let themselves be hired by poor-white trash." (Hurston, 8) Lucy's parents and siblings told her she was throwing her life away. Richard Potts drove Lucy the two miles to the church for her wedding, which her brother Jim also attended, but her mother refused to attend. In Mrs. Potts' mind, Lucy was no longer fit to be her daughter.

Lucy wore a homemade silk dress, the material of which she'd purchased with egg money she'd saved. Following the ceremony, John took Lucy to his small cabin on a white man's plantation and there they made their first home together.

Once John became a family man, his longing to better himself grew even stronger. Hearing of a community in Central Florida that was settled and governed by blacks, he left Lucy with their three young children in Alabama and traveled to Florida to investigate. It was no small thing in those days for a black man to travel such a great distance, and it was done with both hardship and sacrifice. To John, it was worth it if he could have his own land on which to support his family.

The all-black community was Eatonville, located a few miles outside of Winter Park, and adjacent to the all-white community of

Maitland, near Lake Maitland. The area had been settled by three veterans of the Union forces who came to Lake Maitland following the Civil War; they had used a black labor force to clear land and build a fort, then persuaded their friends in the North to join them. Eventually the railroad came in, and wealthy whites from the Northern states flocked to settle the area. The wealthy white settlers worked in tandem with their black employees, treating them with dignity and respect. A black mayor and a black town marshal were voted into office for the community of Maitland.

The town marshal, Joe Clarke, began to mull over the idea of an all-black town. While Clarke was confident it could succeed, other blacks were not so sure that they could effectively govern themselves. The white town leaders thought it a fine idea, however, and offered to assist. Captain Eaton and Captain Lawrence, two of the founders of Maitland, purchased land a mile west of Maitland and donated it for the town site. They also helped to fund the erection of a church building and a hall for general assemblies. To that was added a library with books donated by the white community. The town, named Eatonville after Captain Eaton, received its charter of incorporation on August 18, 1886. As the community grew and prospered, its fame spread throughout the Southern states.

John Hurston spent a year in Eatonville, working and getting settled before sending for Lucy and the children. Lucy brought only a few possessions with her, including her bedstead, her featherbed, and a few quilts.

The Hurstons purchased property, built a sturdy house, and planted gardens and orchards to provide plentiful food for the children that continued to be added to the family, a fact of which John was dutifully proud. He was also proud of the fact that his wife never had to leave her house to work for another person. Life was indeed better than it had been in their sharecropping days.

Eventually Lucy gave birth to Zora Neale Hurston, the fifth of their eight children. Zora's birth records have never been found, so the year has long been in dispute. In later years Hurston claimed to be younger than she actually was, further confusing the facts. It's known with certainty that her birth took place on January 7, which was hog-killing time in Central Florida. According to Hurston's autobiography *Dust Tracks on a Road*, people were busy either butchering their hogs, or assisting neighbors in butchering their's. Lucy was totally alone when Zora was born; she'd sent the smaller children to fetch Aunt Judy, the midwife, but the baby wouldn't wait. A white landowner who had stopped by with a ham helped Lucy with the newborn. Later the man took an interest in young Zora, taking her on fishing excursions and offering advice.

Zora's sister Sara was a favorite of John's and he had no desire for a second girl in the family. Sara was a good, quiet, little girl who never caused problems for anyone; Zora, on the other hand, was curious, imaginative, and adventuresome. "I was always asking," Hurston said later, "and making myself a crow in a pigeon's nest." (Hurston, 24)

The Hurston children were well cared for during Zora's early years. The five-acre garden produced all the vegetables a family with eight children could possibly consume, and the orchard produced oranges, grapefruit, tangerines, and guavas. There was always fish or chicken on the table and a surplus of eggs. The younger children boiled eggs in the iron tea kettle and then lay around the yard, eating their fill and throwing the left over eggs at one another.

Lucy dutifully taught her children their lessons, working on grammar and arithmetic until they had the basics down pat. Eventually the older children taught the younger, but always under Lucy's close supervision. Lucy kept her children close to home, which she thought was more respectable. The eight-room house and the property, she felt, gave them plenty of space to play in, and they had plenty of siblings to play with—there was no reason to go elsewhere. On moonlit summer nights, many of the village children were in the Hurston's yard, playing boisterous games.

The yard did not satisfy Zora, who wondered what might lay at the end of the world. At the age of six or seven she made careful plans with her friend Carrie to run away and find out, but when the time came to leave, Carrie backed out. Zora's disappointment put a crimp in their friendship, and Zora never stopped dreaming about leaving home and traveling to the ends of the world. One year, when her father asked his children what they wanted for Christmas, Zora said she wanted a saddle horse. She figured if she had a horse, she could easily travel to find the end of the world. Her request angered her father, who accused her of always "trying to wear de big hat." (Hurston, 29)

The Hurston house was situated near the road to Orlando, and the imaginative Zora found another way to travel, at least for short distances.

Zora enjoyed sitting atop the gatepost, watching the traffic go by, and when she attracted the attention of white travelers, she sometimes asked if she could travel a ways with them. A few actually stopped and let her ride a half mile or so before she asked to be let out, and walked home. She might have received a whipping for her brashness if she were caught, but that didn't stop Zora, who wanted more than the safe Hurston home and the safe village of Eatonville. Her mother often said that some enemy of Zora's must have sprinkled "travel dust" around the doorstep on the day she was born.

John Hurston often tried to rein Zora in by telling her that her sassy and forward ways were going to bring her nothing but trouble. He continually asked her why she couldn't be more quiet and obedient, like her older sister Sara. Lucy disagreed, saying she didn't want to "squinch" Zora's spirit. She encouraged Zora and her other children to "jump at de sun." Hurston wrote, "We might not land on the sun, but at least we would get off the ground."

Store-bought baby dolls suffered much at Zora's hands, who found conventional toys boring. She preferred instead to sit alone under the house and make up great dramas, using her own props for characters. A piece of corn husk became Miss Corn-Shuck; a cake of scented soap from her mother's dresser drawer became Mr. Sweet-Smell; Reverend Door Knob and the Spool People also had adventures invented for them.

Zora first heard the "lying sessions," or the tall tales of her people, on the porch of Joe Clarke's general store, and she stayed as long as possible when sent there on an errand in order to experience the beauty and the poetry of the stories being told. Even though there were two churches and a school in Eatonville, Joe Clarke's store, according to Hurston, was the "heart and spring of the town" (Hurston, 45), where the general run of town gossip was passed around along with the folktales that Zora loved most, tales of "God, Devil, Brer Rabbit, Brer Fox, Sis Cat, Brer Bear, Lion Tiger, Buzzard, and all wood folk [that] walked and talked like natural men." (Hurston, 47) These stories that she allowed to "hang in her ear" as a child were the same stories she would one day return to collect and record.

Although Zora never cared for the rigors of school, she loved to read. When two wealthy Northern white women visited Zora's classroom one day—not unique in itself, as such visits occurred quite often—they heard Zora reading aloud stories she'd read many times before, and took a liking to her. They met privately with Zora the next day, and gave her a hymnbook, a copy of *Swiss Family Robinson*, a book of fairy tales, and—most special of all—a whole roll of pennies. When the women returned home, they sent Zora clothes and still more books. While she was thankful for the clothes, the books meant more to her than anything else.

At about this time in her life, Zora had a series of visions about events which she felt were yet to come, none of them pleasant. They left her unhappy, weighed down with the knowledge that bad things were going to happen to her. The first event occurred when Zora had just turned nine years old. Her safe, secure life was about to change forever.

THE SAD YEARS

Zora's mother traveled back to Alabama to visit family; when she returned home she developed a chest cold that grew progressively worse, and the once-active Lucy took to her bed more often, too weak to do her housework. Hurston states in her autobiography that she was nine years old at the time, but she may have been closer to thirteen.

Early on September 18, Lucy made three specific requests of Zora that went against the longstanding beliefs and customs of her people and her community: not to remove the pillow from beneath her head until she was dead, and not to cover the clock or the mirror. According to tradition, a pillow under the head made dying long and difficult; if the mirror was not covered, the reflection of the dying person might be forever etched there; and if the dying person's spirit looked upon the clock as it departed, the clock was forever ruined.

Zora went outside to play for a while, then re-entered her mother's bedroom to see the women covering the clock and the mirror and taking the pillow away. Zora cried out for them to stop, trying in her childlike way to explain her mother's requests, but her father pulled her away and made her cease her cries.

The moment was almost more than Zora could bear. Her mother had confided in her and trusted her. "She felt that I could and would carry out her wishes," Hurston wrote, "and I had not. And then in that sunset time, I failed her." (Hurston, 64–65) The incident haunted her long into her adult years.

Her older brother Bob was called home from school in Jacksonville, inconsolable because he arrived too late. The entire village gathered for the funeral held at the Macedonia Baptist Church. Following the funeral service, all eight children gathered in the family kitchen—it was the last time they would be together in one place. Lucy had been the glue that held the Hurston family together, and the compass that kept John Hurston on the right path; her death ended forever the cohesiveness of the family.

Shortly thereafter, Bob returned to school, and Sara went with him; when John spent a lot of time away from the house in the following weeks, Zora was sent to join the two older children at school. As her brother Dick drove her in the buggy to the train depot one dark night, she realized that the first of her visions had come to pass: she was leaving the village, bowed down with heavy grief.

Away from home, family, and friends, Zora struggled to fit into her new school and community. For the first time in her life, she became aware that she was black, and that she was different. She was not as welcome in the white-owned stores as she had been in Maitland—nor in their houses. She missed the woods, the lakes, the pine trees, and the animals, but more than anything, she missed the companionship of her mother. Zora had always been a good student, but now she became known for her back talk and her sassy tongue. Because she was younger than the other students, she was simply in the way.

If school was difficult for Zora, it was even more so for her older sister Sara, who had always been John Hurston's favorite child, and who missed Everett, the baby brother she adored. Eventually Sara was allowed to return home, but found it a much different place; she told Zora in a letter that their father had remarried, and that their new stepmother did not want Sara in the house. Taking baby Everett with her, Sara left home and got married.

Without Lucy by his side as his steady anchor, John had quickly gotten himself into a predicament he later regretted. His new wife was not at all what he'd bargained for—having no desire to take care of any of his children, she drove them all away. Zora had never really minded that Sara was her father's pet, and when she saw Sara hurt and rejected, it brought out the fighter in her, an attitude that came to a head a few years later, when Zora got into an all-out physical fight with her stepmother, and brought her father at long last over to his daughter's side.

When Zora's school tuition was not paid, she was put to work scrubbing the stairs and working in the kitchen. She did what she was told and continued to do well in her studies. At the end of the school year, after her brother had left to take a job, she waited for her father to send for her. Weeks passed and still he did not come.

She was eventually called into the school office, where she was informed that her father had asked the school to adopt Zora. Zora was devastated. A school official, a woman Zora had previously been a little afraid of, gave her the money to pay for the boat trip and then the train that would take her the remaining miles to Maitland, and home.

Her grief over the loss of her mother was multiplied when she returned home to the gloomy, unfriendly place that the Hurston home had become. John Hurston, once the tall, proud, snappy dresser loved and admired by all the children, now looked tired, beaten, and stoop-shouldered. He would eventually lose the respect of the villagers and the parishioners in his church, because no one could tolerate the antics of his new wife.

The next few years were miserable ones for Zora. The four older Hurston children had left home, and the four younger children found themselves passed among friends and relatives. In school only briefly, Zora saw opportunities slipping away from her. Not only was she bereft of love and family, but she also had no books to read. Poverty, which had heretofore been a stranger to her, was now her constant companion. As she herself confessed, she did not know how to be humble, and did not submit well to authority.

She found positions doing housework, but was released when caught reading the books in the families' libraries, or playing with their children. The mistress of one house was pleased that her children adored Zora and things went well for a time, but their camaraderie angered the head cook, who'd been with the family for many years and had a great deal of clout with the master of the house; Zora once again found herself out of a job.

After she'd gone through many more jobs, her brother Bob sent for her to come and live in his home and go to school. Suddenly Zora had hope again—perhaps the sad, lonely years were ending. As she caught the train, she felt pleasure at leaving her home and moving toward her dreams.

Once again, Zora faced deep disappointment. Bob took Zora aside and explained that he didn't want his wife to think he was pampering

Zora, so he wanted her to help with his children for a while before she started school. Zora loved the children and was happy to have a home again, but her longing to go to school never abated.

During her stay with Bob, Zora was befriended by a white woman whose husband worked as an electrician. She took a caring, sisterly interest in Zora, and when she learned of a possible job opening for a maid to a singer in a traveling operetta company, she encouraged Zora to apply.

Wearing a new dress purchased by her friend, Zora met with the singer at the theater and, to her own amazement, got the job, which paid ten dollars a week. While living with her brother, she'd made nothing at all. Zora never returned to her brother's house. When it came time for the troupe to leave town, Zora stuffed her new suitcase with newspaper so her few belongings would not rattle around and embarrass her, then, with a joy-filled heart, she boarded the train with the cast members and stepped into a new world.

Zora Hurston was the only black person in the troupe, and she became the butt of an endless series of jokes, but all were friendly and made in fun. Soon she became everyone's pet, and she and Miss M, as Hurston referred to her, became fast friends. After eighteen months with the group, Hurston had, as she put it, "loosened up in every joint and expanded in every direction." (Hurston, 102)

One cast member, a Harvard man, kept with him a large collections of books; he loaned to Hurston from his library, appeasing her voracious appetite for reading. She was also introduced to classical music for the first time. Most of the players had trained voices and were musicians as well as singers; Hurston was often included in their lively discussions about music interpretation. More importantly, she once again enjoyed a family setting and acceptance as an equal.

At the end of eighteen months, her employer met a man, fell in love, and announced she was to be married and would be leaving the troupe, which ended Hurston's job. The two parted in Baltimore, and the singer gave Hurston a little extra money and encouraged her to return to school. Hurston claimed in her autobiography that she was alone on the streets, but her sister Sara Hurston Mack lived in Baltimore, and it has been established that Hurston lived in her sister's home for a time.

She waited tables to make a living, but hated being patronized by the customers. She intended to save a little so she could attend school, but there was never any extra to save. At this most inopportune time, Hurston suffered an attack of appendicitis and, without resources, went to the free ward at the hospital. Again, Hurston portrayed the event as one that she faced all alone, with no friends or family nearby. Whether this is totally true is unclear.

It may have been at this moment of uncertainty, as she faced surgery, that she became more determined than ever to finish school, because immediately after her recovery, she enrolled in night school in Baltimore. There, in an English class, she heard Coleridge's "Kubla Khan" read aloud, and it changed her life. The words came alive to her, making her realize that the world of literature was the world for her. "This was my world, I said to myself, and I shall be in it, and surrounded by it, if it is the last thing I do on God's green dirt-ball." (Hurston, 107)

The very next week, she entered the high school department of Morgan College. William Pickens, the dean, arranged for her to work as a live-in companion for the wife of a school trustee. Since she was needed only in the mornings and evenings, she spent a good deal of time in the family library, reading.

Her classmates were some of Baltimore's wealthiest and finest young black people. In contrast, Hurston owned one dress, one change of underwear, and a pair of tan oxfords. What Hurston lacked in finances, she made up for in spunk and self-confidence. Never one to hang her head, she quickly made friends, and her overtures were repaid with kindness and courtesy from her fellow students. One of her friends was Bernice Hughes whose father, Dr. W.A.C. Hughes, was a trustee of the college.

Hurston spent two happy years at Morgan before graduating in 1918. She despised math, but did well in her other subjects. For a time, she considered continuing on at Morgan, where she could easily transfer from the high school to the college. That all changed when she was introduced to Mae Miller, a friend of Bernice Hughes and the daughter of a professor at Howard University in Washington, D.C., who insisted to Hurston that she was truly "Howard Material." (Hurston, 113)

Hurston may have been flattered, but she also entertained many doubts. Howard was a well-known, swanky black college complete with fraternities and sororities. The encouragement of her friends overrode her doubts and she moved to Washington, D.C. the summer following her graduation.

She had learned to manicure nails while traveling with the operetta troupe, and now she put that knowledge to good use, working at the G Street shop of George Robinson. Here she held the hands of senators, cabinet members, congressmen, bankers, and journalists as she did their nails week after week. Most of the customers learned that she was working her way through school and tipped her generously.

Hurston was enamored with Howard University and came close to worshiping her instructors. In college assemblies, the singing of the Alma Mater became an emotional moment for her. "My soul stood on tiptoe," she wrote, "and stretched up to take in all that it meant." (Hurston, 115) As a small-town country girl, she knew how privileged she was to be in their midst.

As she finished up her prep courses and moved into the college courses, Hurston met Herbert Sheen, a medical student from Illinois. The two found they had a great deal in common and began spending much of their free time together. Even after Sheen moved to New York in 1921, the two remained in touch. After a time in New York, he transferred to Chicago, where he attended medical school. It was understood that one day they would marry, but Hurston would never be the type of woman who wasted time pining for her man—she stayed active and busy in Sheen's absence.

Her writing was noticed during the year and a half she spent at Howard. She was accepted as a member of the Stylus, a campus literary club formed by a young professor, Alain Leroy Locke, that was limited to seventeen chosen students and two faculty members, and she contributed articles to the paper *The Hill Top*.

Charles S. Johnson, editor of the newly-formed *Opportunity* magazine in New York, happened to notice Hurston's work in *The Hill Top*, and published two of her stories. Johnson, a veteran of World War I, was the principal author of *The Negro in Chicago: A Study of Race Relations and a Race Riot*, published in 1919. By 1921, he was in New York City working for the National Urban League as its national director before becoming editor of the League's new magazine *Opportunity: A Journal of Negro Life*. Johnson used the magazine to attract, encourage, and support young black writers and artists.

Hurston won first prize for a short story in a writing contest sponsored by *Opportunity*, and was invited to the first Award Dinner held on May 1, 1925. It was because of Charles Johnson and *Opportunity* magazine that Zora Hurston found herself living in New York in the midst of the Harlem Renaissance.

HARLEM RENAISSANCE

In a span of just over a decade—from 1920 to the early 1930s—an unprecedented outflow of creative activity by the black community occurred in the Harlem District of New York City. It began in the arena of literature, springing from a series of literary discussions in lower Manhattan (Greenwich Village) and upper Manhattan (Harlem). During this time, groups of talented black writers produced a sizable body of literature in the genres of poetry, fiction, drama, and essay. However, the movement quickly spilled over into music (particularly jazz, spirituals, and blues), art and painting, and dramatic revues and created a deep sense of racial consciousness. The movement was called "The New Negro Movement," but later became known as the Harlem Renaissance.

Harlem was a city within a city, and became the undisputed cultural capital of black America. Harlem in the twenties was made up of black workers, black professionals, black business owners, black property owners, and even a few black judges. The more popular the place became, the more blacks were attracted to it, until eventually the population of the area exceeded two hundred thousand.

Several existing national and international events helped spawn this movement. One was the Great Migration, where thousands of blacks moved from the South to Northern industrialized cities, changing their image from rural to urban. Harlem became the crossroads of that transmigration. The second event was World War I, which ended in 1918, a war in which thousands of young black men sacrificed their lives on the battlefields. Those who survived arrived home with a new spirit of pride and self-determination.

Men like W.E.B. Du Bois and James Weldon Johnson were key figures in the growth of the movement. Du Bois, one of the founders of the National Association for the Advancement of Colored People, scholar and activist, encouraged blacks to "loose the tremendous emotional wealth of the Negro and the dramatic strength of his problem through writing, the stage, pageant, and other forms of art. We should resurrect forgotten ancient Negro art and history, and we should set the black man before the world as both a creative artist and a strong subject for artistic treatment." (Bloom, ed., 50)

James Weldon Johnson, a native Floridian like Hurston, served as field secretary for the NAACP. As journalist, publisher, diplomat, educator, poet, and novelist, he became another of the prime movers of the Harlem Renaissance. Like Charles Johnson, he encouraged African-American writers to undertake more ambitious literary endeavors.

It was into this world of educated and purpose-driven blacks that Hurston arrived in January, 1925. With the intent to complete her education in New York City, she arrived "with $1.50, no job, no friends, and a lot of hope." (Hurston, 122) She located the Charles Johnson family, who befriended her, with Mrs. Johnson giving her carfare and encouragement whenever needed. However, it did not take the feisty Hurston long to make all the right connections with important people. At the *Opportunity* awards banquet, attended by more than three hundred of the key Harlem personalities—as well as at subsequent dinners held at Charles Johnson's home—Hurston knew how to work a crowd and did so with grace and ease.

After making the acquaintance of white novelist Fanny Hurst, Hurston was hired as Hurst's live-in secretary, despite the fact that Hurston was a poor typist and had no head for detailed work. Eventually Hurston was fired as secretary but kept on as chauffeur and companion—an arrangement that worked out well for both.

In an article penned after Hurston's death, Fanny Hurst claimed that Hurston possessed *splendor*. "It irradiated her work and her personality." Zora Hurston "lived laughingly, raffishly, and at least in the years I knew her, with blazing zest for life." Hurst then added, "But regardless of race, Zora had the gift of walking into hearts." (Bloom, ed. 22, 23)

With those innate abilities, Hurston took Harlem by storm. Of all the emerging young artists, she was by far the most outgoing and witty. It was Hurston who coined the term *Niggerati*, and then dubbed herself "Queen of the Niggerati." She loved to give parties and entertain by telling stories she'd learned on the front porch of Joe Clarke's store in Eatonville. Her guests might be treated with fried okra or cooked Florida eels.

When Hurston moved into her own apartment with no furniture and no money, within a few days "it had been completely furnished by her friends with everything from decorative silver birds, perched precariously atop the linen closet, to a footstool for the living room." (Hemenway, 44)

During these years in New York, Hurston became interested in studying black folklore. While other black writers were depicting their people in their urban settings, Hurston looked inward to her rural roots to learn more about the birth of the blues, the folktale, and the spiritual. Few of her Harlem colleagues had the benefit of her rural upbringing in the deep South and thus she was one of the few to understand the richness of her racial heritage. In order to do it justice, she found she would have to turn to the professional study of folklore.

The prosperity of the 1920s brought forth a number of wealthy white patrons who took black artists under their wing to support and promote them. The practice almost became a fad of the times. Hurston met one such woman at the *Opportunity* awards dinner. Annie Nathan Meyer, a novelist and one of the founders of Barnard College, the women's division of Columbia University, was impressed by Hurston and decided to further her education. She arranged for Hurston to be enrolled in Barnard in the fall of 1925. For the first time in many years, Hurston had no financial worries. At that time, Zora Neale Hurston was the only black student enrolled at Barnard College.

Up until that moment, Hurston had been immersed in writing and literature—as far as she was concerned, that would consume her life, and so she embarked upon literary studies at Barnard. This changed after she handed in a paper in an elective course in anthropology. Her professor was so impressed, she showed the paper to Dr. Franz Boas of the Department of Anthropology of Columbia University. Boas encouraged Hurston to redirect her ambitions.

The study of anthropology allowed Hurston to hold a more detached and objective view of her people. Previously, they had been colorful characters for her fiction; now they were scientific objects to be studied for whatever academic value they held. Hurston "had lived Afro-American folklore before she knew that such a thing existed as a scientific concept or had special value ... Hurston came to know that her parents and their neighbors perpetuated a rich oral literature without self-consciousness, a literature illustrating a creativity seldom recognized and almost universally misunderstood." (Hemenway, 22) As the sophistication of anthropological study grew more attractive to Hurston, the appeal of imaginative literature began to fade.

Hurston came to worship Franz Boas just as she had her other instructors, and she worked very hard to please him. In her autobiography, she referred to him as the "king of kings," writing, "That man can make people work the hardest with just a look or a word, than anyone else in creation." (Hurston, 123) The awe she experienced at Barnard exceeded what she'd felt at Howard. Only she knew and understood how far she'd come to be in that place at that time.

During the time that Hurston pursued her studies as the only black student at Barnard, blacks continued to be lynched in record numbers throughout the nation. She did not, however, feel it was her duty or her place to speak out against racism, noting that she was "thoroughly sick" of the race problem. For this stance, she would later be severely criticized.

In the summer of 1926, she joined with other members of the artistic community, notably Langston Hughes and Wallace Thurman, to create a literary magazine they called *Fire!* In their idealism, they saw the magazine as being purely literary, largely unconcerned with sociological problems. The idea for the magazine came from all-night meetings spent at the rooming house where Hughes and Thurman lived. Originally, it was agreed that the various editors, of whom Hurston was one, would pitch in fifty dollars for the expenses. Past that, they hoped to convince interested patrons to take care of the remaining costs. The plan was shaky at best, and by summer's end, they were deeply in debt for the printing costs. Thurman, who'd signed off on the printing bill, paid on it for years afterward.

It was their hope and plan to shock readers. "We want *Fire* to be provocative," Thurman wrote, "want it to provide the shocks necessary to encourage new types of artistic interest and new types of artistic energy." (Hemenway, 49) That plan worked no better than the plan to generate finances. The first issue (as it would turn out, the only issue) featured two of Hurston's works, the play *Color Struck* and a short story, "Sweat," both of which gave her broader recognition and wider acclaim.

Just prior to her graduation from Barnard, she was told by Dr. Boas that she was to receive a fellowship which would finance a trip into the South to collect black folklore. The $1,400 fellowship, arranged by Boas, came through the Carter Woodson's Association for the Study of

Negro Life and History. She also learned she had been admitted to the American Folk-Lore Society, the American Ethnological Society, and the American Anthropological Society—all of which meant a great deal to the young student.

Setting out on her journey in late February 1927, she used the opportunity to contact some of her siblings, starting with Bob, who was now a physician living in Memphis. She and Bob reconciled, and she learned the whereabouts of the others. Benjamin was studying to be a pharmacist and would eventually open a pharmacy in the same building that housed Bob's practice. Clifford Joel was a high school principal in Decatur, Alabama. Everett, the youngest, had become a postal clerk in Brooklyn, New York, and Dick was a chef. "I felt the warm embrace of kin and kind," she said of this interval, "for the first time since the night after my mother's funeral." (Hurston, 125)

Hurston's first attempt at field work was a dismal failure. Realizing too late that her approach was all wrong, she had to return to New York with "my heart beneath my knees and my knees in some lonesome valley. I stood before Papa Franz and cried salty tears." (Hurston, 128) Later she admitted that the "glamour of Barnard College was still upon me ... I knew where the material was all right. But, I went about asking in carefully accented Barnardese." She didn't get enough material, she said, to "make a flea a waltzing jacket." (Hurston, 128)

One detail not written up in her reports after her return to New York was the fact that she had stopped off in St. Augustine, Florida, where she and Herbert Sheen, her fiancé of six years, were married. The marriage was a failure from the outset, for Hurston had no intention of laying aside her work to follow her husband in his career. Years later, in a letter, she would assure him that she loved him deeply, but at the present moment she was anxious to get on with her work. The two were formally separated by January 1928, and were divorced in July of 1931. In a letter to a friend following the divorce, Hurston wrote, "He [Herbert] was one of the obstacles that worried me." (Hemenway, 94)

Before the fellowship was completed and while Hurston was still in Florida, she was instructed by Carter Woodson to undertake research unrelated to folklore. Since Woodson held the purse strings to the fellowship, Hurston had no choice but to do as she was told. Much of the work consisted of transcribing historical documents, which proved to be boring indeed to a free spirit like Hurston.

The last assignment given by Woodson took Hurston to Alabama, where she was to interview Cudjo Lewis—supposedly the only survivor of the last-known slave ship to come to America. The resulting essay "Cudjo's Own Story of the Last African Slaver" appeared in the October 1927 issue of the *Journal of Negro History*.

Almost fifty years after the essay was published—long after Hurston's death—it was discovered that she had fleshed out the article with plagiarized passages from *Historic Sketches of the Old South* by Emma Landon Roche. It's not clear what made her commit such an act; possibly the pressure she was under, along with her doubt that she would be able to produce a scholarly work, prompted her to do it. She never again plagiarized the work of others and went on to produce a great deal of original work.

When Hurston drove back to New York, she had her friend Langston Hughes as a passenger in her car. The two had run into one another in Mobile, Alabama. They took a leisurely route for their return, making several stops so Hurston could collect more folklore along the way. For Hughes, who'd grown up in the North, this was his first introduction to the black folklore of the Deep South.

After her return to New York, Hurston was given the chance to rectify the bitter failure of her first field expedition. Her second chance came through the auspices of Mrs. Rufus Osgood Mason, a woman who would have a powerful impact on Hurston's life and her career.

GODMOTHER

Charlotte van der Veer Quick (Mrs. Rufus Osgood) Mason, a wealthy white Park Avenue dowager, was known for supporting any art that "smacked of primitivism," (Howard, 22) and the artists who produced it. Years earlier she'd lived among tribes of American Plains Indians while financing the work of another of her protégés.

Mason was already a surrogate parent to several artists, one of whom was Hurston's writer friend, Langston Hughes. It's believed that Hughes may have introduced Hurston to Mason. Throughout the twenties, Mason poured thousands of dollars into young African-American artists and, as with any benefactor, she expected something in return. She wanted her gifts to be kept secret, she wanted control over all the artistic work, and she wanted control over the protégés themselves.

When Mason first met Hurston, she was quite taken with the young writer, which resulted in several subsequent meetings. On December 1, 1927, Hurston signed a contract of employment with Mason that would finance her field work for the entire next year. The contract was signed, witnessed, and notarized. She was to be paid $200 per month and would be furnished with a car and a movie camera. In return she would present to Mason all of the materials she collected. Furthermore, Mason would have the right to determine what parts of the material Hurston could use in her books and her revues. Every expenditure down to the penny was to be accounted for and turned in to Mrs. Mason. While the agreement with Mason, whom Hurston was to call "Godmother," was one of almost total dependence, it enabled Hurston to do the fieldwork and gather the materials that would make her famous as a folklorist.

The control that Mason exerted over her artists cannot be underestimated. Langston Hughes saw her as "an amazing, brilliant, powerful personality. I was fascinated by her, and I loved her." (Hemenway, 107) When in later years Hughes broke away from Godmother, the act made him physically ill. Hurston purported that Godmother could read her mind, that a letter from Mason would reach her and address exactly what was happening at the moment. "Her tongue was a knout, cutting off your outer pretenses," Hurston wrote, "and bleeding your vanity like a rusty nail." (Hurston, 129)

Other recipients of Mason's support also testified that they experienced psychic moments with their benefactor. It was known that Mason kept her recipients in subservient positions. When invited to her home they were seated on low footstools while she sat on a higher chair looking down upon them. At age forty, Alain Locke was referred to by Mason as her "precious brown boy." (Wall, 154)

Given the time and the circumstances, Hurston could hardly be faulted for accepting the funding and submitting to the powers Mason held over her. Without it, Hurston's extensive work would likely never have been completed and published.

On her second journey South as a professional anthropologist, Hurston was much wiser. She started her work in Polk County, Florida, in the midst of the logging camps of the Everglades Cypress Lumber

Company. There she won the confidence of the locals and explained her nice car and clothes by saying she was a bootlegger's woman on the run. For more than two months, she did some of her most intensive collecting of stories, songs, lies, and sayings. By cleverly befriending a woman called Big Sweet, she gained what amounted to a personal bodyguard. Eventually Lucy, a knife-wielding woman in a jook joint, frightened Hurston enough that she departed for safer environs.

Leaving Polk County, she returned to Eatonville for a time before moving on to New Orleans, where she planned to investigate hoodoo and the art of conjuring. Throughout the trip, she kept an ongoing correspondence with Langston Hughes. The two discussed matters that could not be discussed in the hearing of Godmother. Hurston shared her ideas for publication of the materials she was gathering, even though she knew none would be published without Mrs. Mason's consent and approval.

The two also discussed the idea of what they called a Negro art theater. Originally, the idea seemed to be Hurston's, but she admitted she always saw Langston as being an integral part of it. In a letter to Hughes, she wrote, "Of *course*, you know I didn't dream of that theatre as a one man stunt. I had you helping 50–50 from the start. In fact, I am perfectly willing to be 40 to your 60 since you are always so much more practical than I. But I know it is going to be *glorious!*" (Hemenway, 115) The idea, of course, had to be kept secret from Mrs. Mason.

Hurston arrived in New Orleans in August, in the worst of the summer heat. While there, she became a part of the hoodoo world in order to collect the information she felt was necessary to complete her work. She learned conjure routines and went through various initiations. With great courage and determination, she allowed herself to become part of a ritual demanding that she lie for sixty-nine hours, face downward and naked, with her navel against a snakeskin lying beneath her. What psychic experiences may have happened during those hours only she knows, but the event altered her life. Such intense involvement demonstrates the lengths to which Hurston was willing to go to gather authentic material.

Upon her return to Florida, she rented a house in Eau Gallie, a town near St. Augustine. There she began to sort through and organize her materials. The dilemma of how to present such a vast amount of information was beginning to weigh heavily on her.

While in Florida, she chanced to hear the music of the Bahamian blacks. Because it had more of an African sound than any other black music she'd heard, she was immediately fascinated. She sailed for the Bahamas before Godmother could protest her leaving. The trip was no disappointment. The Bahamian, she felt, was the greater songster. "He is more prolific and his tunes are better," she wrote. "Nothing is too big, or little to be 'put in sing.' They only need discovery." (Hurston, 143) After gathering hundreds of these songs, she became enamored with the idea of presenting their music to the world.

During her stay in Nassau in 1929, she survived a five-day hurricane, which must have been terrifying but received only a short paragraph in her autobiography—more important to Hurston than surviving a hurricane was the materials she had collected. She distinctly remembered the stench of death in the place.

By March of 1930, Hurston was living near Langston Hughes in Westfield, New Jersey. The two of them were working on their separate projects, still under the control and funding of Mrs. Mason, while also working jointly on a musical comedy based on one of Hurston's short stories which they entitled "Mule Bone, a Comedy of Negro Life." By this time Mason knew of the collaboration and was aiding in the work, providing a typist by the name of Louise Thompson. At first the three of them—Hughes, Hurston, and Thompson—worked well together. Hurston kept them constantly laughing as she acted out various parts in her exuberant manner. As time wore on, however, Hurston came to resent Thompson, and perhaps not without good reason. Both Mrs. Mason and Hughes put more stock in Thompson than that merited by a mere typist.

As summer approached, Hurston took her part of the play and left for the South. When she returned in the fall, her attitude toward Hughes had cooled considerably. Perhaps because of her anger over Thompson being included as a collaborator, not only by Hughes, but by Mrs. Mason as well, Hurston filed for sole authorship of the play.

To further complicate matters, Hughes was growing increasingly dissatisfied under Mason's stringent control of his work. Hurston may have wanted to distance herself from this rift, hoping their benefactor would not take her wrath out on Hurston. By December, Langston Hughes had made a break from Mason. The parting scene was bitter and he was ill for weeks.

By January 15, Hughes, now living in Cleveland with his mother, learned that Hurston was distributing copies of *Mule Bone* with her name as author. He immediately sent his version of the play off to be copyrighted in both names, after which he threatened Hurston with litigation. Eventually, after Hughes had procured an attorney through the NAACP, he received a letter from Hurston wherein she expressed her resentment of Thompson being added as a third party.

For a time it seemed as though the rift would be smoothed over. Through Hughes's connections, the play was scheduled to be produced in Cleveland by the Gilpin Players. However, when Hurston arrived in Cleveland, she learned that Louise Thompson had been there as well. Suspecting the worst, Hurston flew into a rage and accused Hughes of double-crossing her, and the production was called off. In truth, Thompson had been in Cleveland for reasons other than the play. The separation of Hurston and Hughes became permanent, with neither forgiving the other. Although the play had been Hurston's original work, it was difficult to ascertain who wrote which parts. For years the play lay neglected, but was finally performed in February 1991 at the Lincoln Center in New York City, sixty years after their falling out.

As fate would have it, Hurston's break with Godmother came only a short time after her final break with Hughes. By 1931 the country was beginning to feel the crunch of the Depression, and the glittering days of the Harlem Renaissance were over. The decade of the twenties had been a time of coming out for Hurston, and a time when she'd grown more deeply committed to her life's work.

By the early thirties, Hurston was driven by a passion to present the music of her people in its truest form. Through her intense work in the field, she'd come to know firsthand the difference between what she called the singing of "genuine" spirituals and "neo-spirituals." The latter, she asserted, were "all good work and beautiful, but *not* the spirituals." Genuine spirituals, she said, "are Negro religious songs, sung by a group, and a group bent on expression and not on sound effects." She went on to add, "There has never been a presentation of genuine Negro spirituals to any audience anywhere." (Hemenway, 55) Hurston desperately wanted to rectify that situation. Hurston's work in this area was often misunderstood, even by her closest friends and cohorts, but the lack of support never slowed her down, nor did it cool her enthusiasm.

Hurston had an opportunity to voice her feeling in the matter of black music by way of Nancy Clara Cunard, the only child of English baronet Sir Bache Cunard and his American wife, and heiress to the famed Cunard Shipping Lines. Nancy grew up in England and Paris surrounded by servants and governesses. In Paris she met Henry Crowder, a black American jazz musician, who introduced Nancy to the American civil rights movement, after which she determined to create a volume of work to record the history of blacks in America. The resulting book, an anthology of black literature entitled *Negro*, was published at Nancy Cunard's expense and released in 1934, after long years of work. While some blacks, such as Langston Hughes, refused to be a part of the work, Hurston's contributions amounted to seven articles, the most noted of which was titled "Spirituals and Neo-Spirituals."

In March 1931, Mrs. Mason formally severed Hurston's contract at the time when Hurston was struggling to write *Mules and Men*. The sudden lack of finances created a terrible strain. Not knowing where else to turn, she found herself continually contacting Mrs. Mason, asking for money to tide her over. However painful the separation was, Hurston for the first time in five years no longer had to answer to Godmother. She was free to do her own work in her own way.

Spirituals On Stage

In spite of the unhappy ending over *Mule Bone*, Hurston had never been so close to seeing the dramatic part of her dreams fulfilled. She couldn't get the thought of drama and stage productions out of her head. She'd detested the "darkies" musicals produced by whites, and she never fully accepted the arranged musicals done by all-black choirs. With *Mule Bone* now a dead dream, she turned her attention to the possibility of presenting a revue to the world that showed black music in its most natural settings.

She assisted producer Forbes Randolph in a revue called *Fast and Furious*, advertised as a "colored revue in thirty-seven scenes." (Howard, 25) She not only wrote several sketches, but also played the part of a pompom girl, which gave her the chance to be on stage. The show folded after one night. Hurston was paid $75 after she had been told she might take in as much as $500. After *Fast and Furious*, she became involved in yet another revue called *Jungle Scandals*, which also saw a very short run.

Searching for an open door that would allow her work to be produced on the stage, she put together selections from the music she had collected and submitted them to Hall Johnson, the most famous choral director in the country at that time. He returned them to her, saying that the world was not ready for such "barbaric melodies and harmonies." (Hemenway, 177)

Such a rejection served only to spur Hurston into action. Shortly after receiving Johnson's letter, she recruited a group of performers and started rehearsals in her own apartment. The revue consisted of "Bahamian dances to worksongs, children's games, conjure ceremonies, and jook scenes." (Hemenway, 177)

The finished show, entitled *The Great Day*, was presented to Hall Johnson who at first agreed to work with Hurston on the project but later changed his mind. When his production *Run Little Chillun* came out, the grand finale was staged exactly like the finale of *The Great Day*. Although Hurston claimed that Johnson stole her material, she was unable to fight against him.

Incensed, Hurston again turned to Mrs. Mason for help to produce her own show. Here was her opportunity to present the authentic culture of her people, and she was willing to sacrifice anything to make it happen. Pouring herself into the project, she admitted that she had "worked harder on this than anything else except collecting it." (Hemenway, 178) The material for the show covered a day in a lumber camp similar to that which she visited in Polk County, Florida. The advertisement for the revue boasted that the material had not been influenced by "Harlem or Broadway," which was true. With Mason's help, the show was presented Sunday, January 10, 1932, at the John Golden Theater.

While the show brought favorable reviews, the intake did not cover expenses. When all was tallied, Hurston still owed money and again turned to Godmother to make up the difference. In spite of everything, Hurston knew that she'd accomplished what she set out to do, and that she'd done something no one else had ever done—or dared to do. Her one hope was that a Broadway producer might take enough interest in the show to fund the production. That never happened. A letter to Mrs. Mason only hints at the despair Hurston suffered, stating she felt "too keenly conscious of how far short I fell of the mark at which I aimed." (Howard, 26)

Hurston made desperate attempts to hold her group together despite being unable to pay them. New York audiences were able to view the production one more time when *The Great Day* was presented for the School for Social Research at the Vanderbilt Hotel on March 29, 1932. The troupe then disbanded, not without a number of disputes over unpaid salaries.

It would be difficult to measure the tremendous stress under which Hurston worked to produce her revue. Just being black and a woman in that day and time would have been obstacle enough. Add to that the fact that she had little or no funds to pay her actors and cover expenses for a work that she alone believed in, placing her in a very lonely position. And the person from whom she was forced to borrow—Mrs. Mason—held a great abhorrence toward anything that had to do with actors and the theater. Mrs. Mason also held control over almost all of Hurston's materials.

Not surprisingly, the intestinal problems that had plagued Hurston most of her life flared up during this period. In response to her continual complaints of pain, Mrs. Mason arranged for Hurston to be seen by a well-known specialist in Brooklyn.

Her arrival obviously surprised the receptionist and the nurse, who separated her from the others in the waiting room, and asked her to wait in what appeared to be the room where the dirty laundry was kept. When the doctor finally came to her, he "went through some motions" of an examination, after which she left the office thoroughly disgruntled. She later wrote about the experience and entitled it "My Most Humiliating Jim Crow Experience." (Walker, ed., 163–4)

By the time spring arrived, Hurston yearned to return to the South, and turned once again to Mrs. Mason for the money. In Eatonville she found her strength and vigor renewed and was able to begin work on *Mules and Men* right away, at last completing the manuscript that had been her work-in-progress for a number of years in the fall of 1932. As soon as she laid it aside, her mind turned once again to the production of her revue.

Rollins College, located in the neighboring town of Winter Park, seemed the best place to begin. Since 1925, Rollins had been under the leadership of President Hamilton Holt, a nationally recognized journalist and editor. Holt was a forward-looking educator instituting a tradition of experimental education at the college.

A year prior to Hurston's return to Florida, the college had hosted a national Curriculum Conference with the distinguished educator John Dewey as chairman. Following the conference the school established a number of educational innovations, so much so that when Sinclair Lewis accepted the Nobel Prize in Literature, he mentioned Rollins as being one of the colleges in the United States doing the most to encourage creative work in contemporary literature.

It's highly probable that Hurston was familiar with, and encouraged by, this liberal leadership when she wrote to the school, describing her revue and inquiring if they might be interested in supporting such a production. She succeeded in gaining the interest of Robert Wunsch of the English department, who told her the school was willing to help put on the production.

Rollins provided some funding and, by her sheer exuberance, Hurston was able to recruit cast members from nearby Eatonville. By January 1933, they were ready for production. Under its new title, *From Sun to Sun*, the revue was a hit with white Southern audiences and was presented again in February—but no blacks were allowed in the audiences in pre-integration America. In a letter to Mrs. Mason, Hurston explained how she tried to have a space set aside for blacks, "but find that there I come up against solid rock." (Hemenway, 185)

From Sun to Sun played in a number of Florida towns, and eventually was produced in Eatonville itself, much to the delight of its citizens.

Lack of finances continued to be a problem for Hurston, and her desperate need for money drove her back to writing. In August, after the production of *From Sun to Sun*, her short story "The Gilded Six-Bits" came to the attention of Bertram Lippincott, which in turn brought her the surprise telegram offering her a contract for *Jonah's Gourd Vine*.

Hurston's first novel appeared in May 1934 to mixed reviews. Many who reviewed the book completely missed the point and its purpose. *The New York Times* noted that the preacher's sermon in the novel "is too good, too brilliantly splashed with poetic imagery to be the product of any one Negro preacher." (Howard, 34)

This type of misunderstanding of her people was especially difficult for Hurston to endure. In a letter to her friend James Weldon

Johnson, she noted that only the two of them realized that "there are hundreds of preachers who are equaling that sermon weekly. He [the reviewer] does not know that merely being a good man is not enough to hold a Negro preacher in an important charge. He must also be an artist. He must be both a poet and an actor of a very high order, and then he must have the voice and figure." (Howard, 34)

Nevertheless, the book did well and was even chosen for the Book-of-the-Month Club for May. It is important to note that Hurston's best works were published at a time when Americans had the lowest amount of expendable income. The number of book-buying consumers had dwindled considerably because of the Depression; otherwise, her royalties might have amounted to a great deal more.

Between completion of the novel and its release, Hurston sought some way to earn a living. When Mary McLeod Bethune, president of Bethune-Cookman College in Daytona Beach, contacted her and suggested that Hurston come to the college to establish a school of dramatic arts, Hurston was definitely interested. She moved to Daytona Beach in January 1934, but the Bethune experience proved to be disappointing. Both Hurston and Bethune were strong, independent women. Bethune felt that her authority should be law, and Hurston felt that, since she knew more about drama, her suggestions should be accepted and implemented. When Hurston was asked to write a pageant for the school's anniversary from a script written by a faculty member, her opinion of the scriptwriter, who, she said, "had no more idea of drama than I have about relativity" (Hemenway, 201) revealed her frustration.

By the time *Jonah's Gourd Vine* was released, Hurston was ready to quit the Bethune-Cookman Drama department and return to her own work. She took her revue to the National Folk Festival in St. Louis, and her presence at the festival gave her more publicity and helped with book sales as well.

An added advantage of having Lippincott take *Jonah's Gourd Vine* was that it gave Hurston a publisher for *Mules and Men*. Lippincott was delighted to take her second book, and the contract gave her greater financial independence than she'd had for many years.

As she became more independent, she grew further and further away from Mrs. Mason. Still, she could never forget that Godmother's assistance had advanced her career. "If I am acclaimed by the world," she wrote to Alain Locke, "and make a million in money, I would feel still that she was responsible for it." (Hemenway, 204)

In the fall of 1934, Hurston was invited to bring *The Great Day* to Chicago, and renamed it *Singing Steel* for the two-day production. She was housed at the YWCA and paid $500, which in the midst of the Depression was a sizeable amount. When officials from the Julius Rosenwald Foundation viewed *Singing Steel*, they invited Hurston to return to Columbia to study for her Ph.D.

On her way to Chicago, she had spent time at Fisk University in Tennessee, where she had been considered for a teaching position. When the university turned cool and elusive about the matter, it was probably due to the content of her dramatic productions. Their response was true to form, since support for her work from fellow blacks was minimal, at best. Hurston had continually struggled to have her work accepted by members of her own race—many of whom viewed her presentations as much too primitive.

Confused and disappointed at this lack of understanding, she penned an article for the *Washington Tribune* entitled "Race Cannot Become Great Until It Recognizes Its Talents." It was Hurston's purpose to show the world that black folklore was something particularly their own, something that should be a matter of pride for African-Americans.

When the opportunity to teach at Fisk fell through, the invitation to return to Columbia was more appealing—she thought advanced education might give her more credibility. But even as she accepted the scholarship to return to school, she was filled with doubts and confusion. It was important to her that her work be taken seriously, but she did not want the freshness and the vitality of the black folklore to be buried in scientific journals. How she would carry out this conviction was yet to be seen.

WEST INDIAN VOODOO

The first offer from the Rosenwald Foundation was in the amount of $3,000 for two years of study, which would culminate with her receiving her doctorate. However, despite the approval of Dr. Boas, the foundation considered the plans she presented for research and study unacceptable, and the amount was reduced to $700 and the time shortened to a period between December 1, 1934 and June 30, 1935.

Hurston was understandably upset with the change in the amount of funding. She felt it put her back into the position of taking employment while studying. She explained the problem as best she could in a letter to Boas:

> I wonder if it ought not to be taken into consideration that I have been on my own since fourteen years old and went to high school, college ... because I wanted to, and not because I was being pushed? All of these things have been done under most trying circumstances and I stuck. I have had two or three people say to me, why don't you go and take a master's or a doctor's degree in Anthropology since you love it so much. They never seem to realize it takes money to do that. I had such a hard time getting the money to take my bachelor's that I could appreciate what it meant to attempt to attend a college on nothing. Another thing, it is hard to apply oneself to study when there is not money to pay for food or lodging. (Hemenway, 208)

Hurston's relationship with the foundation's president, Edwin Embree, was shaky from the start, as both had different goals in mind. Embree had told Boas that he hoped "the brilliant Miss Hurston" could be "transformed" into a serious student. (Hemenway, 208) He didn't know how elusive his subject could be.

Resorting to her old defense mechanism of doggedly doing her own thing, she informed Embree that the arrangements were agreeable, took the first payment of $100, and hit the road. As she went her way, she gave a number of media interviews to promote *Jonah's Gourd Vine*. Those at the Rosenwald Foundation were soon reading interviews with Hurston in which she stated that she'd just about "decided to pass [up] the proffered Julius Rosenwald Scholarship ... and start in writing a book." She then added, "I have lost all my zest for a doctorate. I have definitely decided that I never want to teach, so what is the use of the degree. It seems that I am wasting two good years of my life when I should be working." (Hemenway, 210)

Once she had put in her few months and collected her $700, Hurston ended her attempts at formal education, which she realized weren't taking her where she wanted to go with her career.

While involved with the Rosenwald scholarship, she had become entangled in a love affair that, together with the poor funding, made for several stressful months. The man, identified in her autobiography only as A.W.P., had a powerful impact on her life. "I did not just fall in love," she wrote, "I made a parachute jump. No matter which way I probed him, I found something more to admire. We fitted each other like a glove." (Hurston, 183) He wanted her to forsake her career for him, and that was something she could never do. They also found it difficult to trust each other.

When Alan Lomax and Mary Elizabeth Barnicle of New York University asked her to join them on a short research trip, she jumped at the chance to get away. The trio, one black and two whites, were an interesting sight in the South. At times, Hurston instructed them to wear blackface—not for the sake of the blacks, but to avoid concern by white officials.

Alan Lomax was the son of the highly-acclaimed folklorist John Lomax, and had worked with his father on previous projects. He clearly thought highly of Zora Hurston, and felt deeply indebted to her for leading him into rich discoveries of black folk music. In a letter to his father, he praised Hurston during their recording experiences in Eatonville:

> They have thronged our house by day and night ever since we have been here. They have been perfectly natural and easy from the first on account of Zora who talks their language and can out-nigger any of them. She swaps jokes, slaps backs, honies up to the men a little when necessary and manages them so that they ask us for no money, but on the other hand cooperate in the friendliest sort of spirit. (Hemenway, 212)

The cooperative efforts might have continued had Hurston not taken a distinct dislike to Barnicle. Hurston decided to stay behind in Florida as Lomax and Barnicle traveled on to the Bahamas.

The fall of 1935 saw the release of *Mules and Men*, a work that had been five or six years in the making. The book's entrance onto the literary scene opened the doors to ongoing criticism and debate over Hurston's work and her approach to the subject of black culture.

On the one hand, reviewers such as those at *The New York Times* pointed out that Hurston encouraged readers to "listen in" while "her own people" were being "natural," something they could never be in the company of outsiders. Those of her own race countered that the book lacked authenticity in that the exploitation, the terrorism, and the misery of the black race were missing. Black author Sterling Brown stated in his review that "the Negro story teller is missing in bitterness ... *Mules and Men* should be more bitter; it would be nearer the total truth." (Hemenway, 219) These points and counterpoints would be typical of the public's reaction to Hurston's work for years to come.

Hurston returned to New York prior to the release of *Mules and Men* and searched for work among the many federal programs of the Works Progress Administration, finding a position with the Federal Theater Project. Her position as a drama coach brought in $23.86 a week, a salary she drew steadily from August 1935 until March 1936 while working mainly with the special Harlem unit of the WPA project. Under her direction, many talented young black theater enthusiasts were trained for the stage production of *Walk Together Chillun*.

It's unknown how long Hurston might have stayed with the WPA, had the offer of a Guggenheim Fellowship not turned her attentions elsewhere. In March, she was offered the opportunity to travel to the West Indies for a year of writing and collecting information on the Obeah Voodoo practices. Since she was still struggling in her bittersweet relationship with A.W.P., she accepted yet another excuse to leave New York City.

Arriving in Kingston, Jamaica, on April 14, she quickly moved into the backcountry, intent on learning as much as she could about the customs there. Her first reaction was one of disbelief and abhorrence at the degree of racial prejudice and male domination. It was the aim in Jamaica to "talk English, act English and *look* English," the last of which, she explained, was the most difficult:

> It's not so difficult to put a coat of European culture over African culture, but it is next to impossible to lay a European face over an African face in the same generation. So everybody who has any hope at all is looking out for the next generation and so on. The color line in Jamaica between the white Englishman and the blacks is not as sharply drawn as

between the mulattoes and the blacks. To avoid the consequences of posterity the mulattoes give the blacks a first class letting alone. There is a frantic stampede white-ward to escape from Jamaica's black mass. (Walker, ed., 125)

Whereas in America anyone with a drop of black blood was considered African-American, in Jamaica anyone with a drop of white blood considered themselves white and were declared to be so even on the census rolls. Hurston wanted to see the blacks of Jamaica begin to respect their own culture, which included songs, stories, dances, and colorful proverbs. Using the same techniques of involvement that she'd used in the southern states, she managed to become a part of local events, not the least of which was an adventurous wild boar hunt. Her research was intensive and thorough, taking her to every parish on the island.

By September 1936, she had traveled from Jamaica to Haiti, where she rented a small house in an isolated spot and spent time writing, when she was not out researching. As with *Mules and Men*, she faced the formidable task of organizing the mass of research materials she'd gathered. When the task grew too strenuous, she turned to other types of writing.

Haiti gave Hurston a sense of peace unlike anything she'd ever experienced. In this environment, she poured out the emotions that had been welling up inside her regarding her doomed love affair. In a matter of a few weeks, she'd written what was to become her most noteworthy novel, *Their Eyes Were Watching God*.

"The plot was far from the circumstances," she admitted, "but I tried to embalm all the tenderness of my passion for him in *Their Eyes Were Watching God*." (Hemenway, 231)

She sent the manuscript to Lippincott, who quickly accepted it, and after little editing scheduled its publication for March, 1937. Meanwhile, Hurston continued her research in Haiti, requesting and receiving a fellowship renewal from the Guggenheim Foundation.

At one point, as she was researching voodoo gods, particularly one whose powers she'd been warned against, she became violently ill. She spent two weeks in bed, and there were moments when she thought she was not going to make it. Shaken by the incident, she stopped her research and spent the remainder of her time in Haiti recovering physically and sightseeing. She returned to New York in September of 1937, in time to take part in the publicity for *Their Eyes Were Watching God.*

White reviewers seemed to like the book, but most missed the point. Her own people, as before, attacked the book as being too primitive, or lacking in social consciousness. Her old friend Alain Locke, writing in the January 1938 issue of *Opportunity,* pointed out that folklore was the book's "main point" and added that it was "folklore fiction at its best." But then he asked pointedly when Hurston was going to "come to grips with motive fiction and social document fiction." (Hemenway, 241)

Even though Locke had often helped Hurston in the past, it hurt her deeply for him to publicly attack her work. In typical Zora Hurston style, she struck back with a response filled with anger, demanding that *Opportunity* publish it. Wisely, they refused. She accused Locke of being one who "lives by quotations trying to criticize people who live by life." (Hemenway, 242)

She left New York and headed home to Florida to work on the book that would contain the material gathered in the West Indies. The book was finished in March, and Lippincott scheduled it to appear the next fall. In the time between the book's completion and its publication, she once again worked for the government through the Federal Writers' Project for the state of Florida—yet another branch of the WPA. Designed to help out-of-work writers during the Depression, the Writers' Project employed many of the well-known writers of the day.

On April 25, 1938, she took the position of editor of the Florida volume of the American Guide series. Never known as a good employee, Hurston often disappeared for weeks at a time, telling no one of her whereabouts. What few people knew at the time was that, while she was away, she was hard at work on her newest book, *Moses, Man of the Mountain.* "Her reputation on the project was that of an actress who loved to show off, a woman of remarkable talent and spirit, a loner, an uncooperative co-worker, an editor who hated to stay inside at her desk." (Hemenway, 252) In spite of her truancy, she stayed with the project for almost a year and a half.

Another project under her direction was *The Florida Negro.* With the money provided for the work, she requisitioned a recording machine from the D.C. offices and traveled to the Florida Everglades for the research. While the manuscript amounted to over two hundred pages, the book was never published.

By the summer of 1939, jurisdiction of the Writers' Project was transferred from federal control to state control. In the midst of the turnover, Hurston left her position. She again began to think about employment at a college. Since her attempts had failed before, it's not clear why she wanted to try again, unless she was seeking a steady income. Although she had published several books, her income from them was never substantial—she'd never received a royalty check for more than $1,000. Unlike her white counterparts in the industry, she did not enjoy the luxury of an active literary agent negotiating the best advances and royalties on her behalf. Hurston represented herself, and she openly admitted that she had no concept of how to manage her money.

After returning to her alma mater of Morgan State to receive an honorary degree in June, she accepted a position with North Carolina College for Negroes in Durham. Following that, she made one more attempt at the state of matrimony. In both situations, she again encountered frustration and disappointment.

THE SEARCH FOR ADVENTURE

Hurston met Albert Price III in Jacksonville, where he was building playgrounds for the WPA. The twenty-three-year-old Price and the thirty-eight-year-old Hurston (if indeed she was that young) married on June 27, 1939, in Ferandina, Florida. Within the year, they were at odds; Hurston accused Price of excessive drinking and Price accused her of trying to put a voodoo spell on him. Price stayed behind in Florida when Hurston took her position at the college in North Carolina. They were formally divorced by 1943.

In true Hurston fashion, she arrived at the college in Durham in her new red convertible and refused to live in campus housing, as required by the president, and instead found a house outside the community. She did little as head of the drama department, complaining that she needed more support from the school. A production of *From Sun to Sun* was scheduled for December, but she canceled it, saying there wasn't enough time to prepare.

The truth was, Hurston was distracted by her acquaintance with Paul Green, a white Southerner from the University of North Carolina in Chapel Hill, who had heard Hurston speak at a meeting of the Carolina Dramatic Association and invited her to attend playwriting classes in his home. They began to talk about collaboration on a play entitled *John de Conqueror*. The thought of playwriting never failed to excite Hurston, and her excitement bubbled over in a letter to Green:

> You do not need to concern yourself with the situation here at the school. I won't care what happens here or if nothing happens here so long as I can do the bigger thing with you. My mind is hitting on sixteen cylinders on the play now ... I see no reason why the firm of Green and Hurston should not take charge of the Negro playrighting [sic] business in America, and I can see many reasons why we should. (Hemenway, 256)

Another distraction was the November release of her book *Moses, Man of the Mountain*. She'd been working on the novel, by far her most ambitious project, for the better part of five years, after first publishing the seed of her idea as a short story.

In her year of teaching at North Carolina College, not one play was produced in the Drama department. She hedged by demanding that courses be offered in playwriting, direction, and production. The school and Hurston reached an impasse, and Hurston left. During the same period, her relationship with Paul Green deteriorated and the promise of collaboration with him faded as well. At loose ends, she moved back to New York, where she contacted old friends and attempted to plan her next writing project.

When her editor Bertram Lippincott suggested that she write her autobiography, she found the idea repugnant at first, because she felt her career was only just beginning. Lippincott talked her into it by saying the book could be the first part of a volume. Hurston's friend Katharine Edson Mershon invited her to visit California, and she used the visit to rest and to work on her autobiography. She found the book a difficult undertaking and much of what she wrote fell short of the whole truth—her age being one of the more obvious misrepresentations.

While in the land of movies, she worked for a short time as a story consultant with Paramount Studios. Early in 1942, however, she left the glitter and glamour of Hollywood to return to St. Augustine, Florida, where she completed her biography. *Dust Tracks on a Road* came out in late November of that same year. *Dust Tracks on a Road* was by far her most popular book in terms of sales, but was again attacked by blacks for the fact that she almost completely omitted any instances of prejudice or racism. In her defense, it must be remembered that the finished product included what her publisher allowed. In an interview she explained, "Rather than get across all of the things which you want to say you must compromise and work within the limitations [of those people] who have the final authority in deciding whether or not a book shall be printed." (Hemenway, 286–7) Her original manuscripts, prior to editing, show a much more confident voice and style than the finished book would offer. The book, generally accepted by white reading audiences, won the *Saturday Review*'s $1,000 Anisfield-Wolf Award.

After the publication of *Dust Tracks on a Road*, the general theme of Hurston's work began to change. As the black spokesperson to whom white publishers turned for comments, she found a market writing articles for the popular slick magazines of her day. The pay was good and the work steady. Two of the articles, "Cock Robin, Beale Street" and "Story in Harlem Slant," gave vivid renditions of the rhythm and music of colloquial slang from blacks both in the North and the South.

While living in St. Augustine during 1943, Hurston became friends with novelist Marjorie Kinnan Rawlings, author of *The Yearling*. Rawlings took an instant liking to Hurston and even invited her new friend to her husband's segregated resort hotel. Being street smart, Hurston knew enough to enter through the kitchen and use the stairs to the Rawlings apartment, after which they had a pleasant visit together.

Always at home in Florida, Hurston purchased a houseboat, named the *Wanango*. The thirty-two-foot cruiser might have had a crowded galley, but she loved it. Not only did she have the solitude she craved, but there appeared to be no segregation on the waterfront: "all the other boat owners are very nice to me," she wrote. "Not a word about race." (Hemenway, 296)

The boat also gave her a degree of independence; no one could evict her from what she owned. Cruising up and down the Halifax River, she could write and fish to her heart's content. She wrote to a friend that she had "achieved one of my life's pleasures by owning at last a houseboat. Nothing to delay the sun in its course ... The Halifax river is very beautiful and the various natural expressions of the day on the river keep me happier than I have ever been before in my life ... Here, I can actually forget for short periods the greed and ultimate brutality of man to man." (Hemenway, 298) The latter comments obviously referred to World War II, which was raging at the time.

Just when life looked serene for Hurston, her attention was turned away once again, this time to the ruins of a Mayan city in Honduras. Reginald Brett, a gold miner from the area, had read *Tell My Horse* and was impressed enough to contact Hurston and suggest that anthropological work in the area could yield great monetary rewards. By her own admission, Hurston was "like a mule in a tin stable. I am pitching, rearing and kicking at the walls." (Hemenway, 301) Hurston wanted to spend two years in Honduras doing research, and planned to get there on the schooner of her waterfront friend, Captain Fred Irvine. Irvine wasn't the most reliable person, and plans for the trip were on again, off again. While she sought funding for such an undertaking, she purchased a newer houseboat, the *Sun Tan*, and finished her book *Mrs. Doctor*.

After submitting *Mrs. Doctor* to Lippincott, Hurston learned that her editors were greatly concerned with the sloppiness of her work. She traveled to New York and had lunch with Bertram Lippincott, who told her that Lippincott had decided not to publish the book. It was her first rejection since she'd started working with the publishing house in 1934, nearly ten years earlier.

She stayed in New York through the winter of 1946–47, but she didn't even look up her old friends. It must have been a miserable time for her—the plans to travel to Honduras were on hold, and now she had no prospect of publication for her book.

In the spring, Marjorie Rawlings urged Hurston to contact Rawlings' own editor, Maxwell Perkins of Scribner's Publishing House. Perkins had a sterling reputation for helping many famous authors, not the least of whom were F. Scott Fitzgerald and Ernest Hemingway. To Hurston's delight, Perkins spoke with her and then purchased the option to contract for her book. This meant she now had the money to go to Honduras. By May, she was in Central America, ready for a new adventure.

Hurston had not been in Honduras long before the country's sky-high inflation hit home—the money she had would not last as long as she'd hoped. To make things worse, Maxwell Perkins died in June and she was turned over to a new editor, Burroughs Mitchell. She wrote panicky letters asking for money and was allowed another $500 against royalties.

There was certainly not enough money to outfit an expedition, so she sat in a noisy hotel and wrote. She deemed her novel ready that fall, and sent it off. By then the rainy season had arrived and prevented any treks into the interior. In February, Scribner's asked that she return to New York to work on the final edits. They even sent money to Hurston for passage to ensure that she would come home.

Spending the summer at the home of a friend, she awaited the October release of her novel. The book, with the final title of *Seraph on the Suwanee*, was a story about white Southerners—her first attempt at writing about whites and, for the first time in her career, a move away from any hint of folklore and the Deep-South idioms that had made her famous.

Her attempt was not successful. Even Hurston was disappointed with how the book turned out. In a letter to Marjorie Rawlings she lamented that she was not sure she had done her best, "but I tried ... I need not tell you that my goal still eludes me. I am in despair because it keeps ever ahead of me." (Hemenway, 315) It would be the last novel she ever published.

The despair she experienced after the publication of *Seraph on the Suwanee* was about to intensify greatly under circumstances beyond her control.

THE WANING YEARS

During the difficult winter of 1946–7, Hurston had lived in an apartment house in Harlem, where she had encountered the emotionally disturbed son of her landlady and, in her usual open manner, suggested to the woman that the boy be taken to Bellevue for psychiatric testing. Evidently, the landlady took the remark as a personal affront. Almost a year later, she filed charges against Hurston for sexually molesting her son.

Officers went to Hurston's apartment on September 13, 1948, arrested her, and took her to police headquarters for questioning. Cries of her innocence went unheeded, as did her request for a lie detector test. Fortunately her publisher was able to obtain an attorney for her, a man named Lewis Waldman.

The boy's testimony revealed that Hurston had been in Honduras during the times he accused her of meeting with him. Waldman presented these discrepancies to the District Attorney, Frank Hogan, who in turn conducted a full-scale investigation and decided that there was not enough evidence to make a case; all charges were dropped.

This experience was stressful, but it was not the end. A black employee of the court leaked the news to the black newspapers. While the white newspapers barely gave the incident a passing glance, black papers blared the accusation in lurid and suggestive headlines. In the national edition of Baltimore's *Afro-American*, readers were shocked to see these words set among other lurid stories: "Boys, 10, Accuse Zora." The subtitle read "Novelist Arrested on Morals Charge. Reviewer of Author's Latest Book Notes Character Is 'Hungry for Love.'"

The newspaper stories were neither factual nor objective. Such betrayal by her own people shattered Hurston. Writing to her friend Carl Van Vechten, she said, "It seemed that every hour some other terror assailed me, the last being the *Afro-American* sluice of filth." (Hemenway, 321) Her letters make it clear that she contemplated suicide. Everything she'd known and trusted in had seemingly failed her:

> All that I have ever tried to do has proved useless. All that I have believed in has failed me. I have resolved to die. It will take a few days for me to set my affairs in order, and then I will go ... no acquittal will persuade some people that I am innocent. I feel hurled down a filthy privy hole. (Hemenway, 322)

In spite of everything, Hurston managed to pull out of the depression, even though its effects were long-lasting. Because most people were unaware of the incident, and in spite of the fact that Southern bookstores refused to carry the book and Hurston was too upset and distracted to work on publicity, sales of her newest book were not adversely affected. The book sold well—it quickly sold through its initial run of three thousand books, and then a second run of two thousand.

As she always did when feeling down, Hurston returned to Florida to soak up the sunshine and allow herself time to heal. She was still considering a trip to Honduras and much of her income at this time was put into preparations, but Irvine, proving as unreliable as ever, was about to lose his boat to bad debts. Finally Hurston's money ran out and she had to seek work as a maid—the work she'd performed as a young woman.

James Lyons, a reporter from the *Miami Herald*, found her and reported his great discovery. Thinking quickly, Hurston told Lyons that she was temporarily "written out" but that she had a novel and three short stories in the hands of her agent. She also said she was planning to start a national magazine by and for domestics, and that she was simply researching to write an article.

In 1951 she did sell an article to the *Saturday Evening Post* for $1,000, making it possible for her to return to Eau Gallie. She moved back into the little house where she'd written the final draft of *Mules and Men* years earlier, and she found happiness and contentment in the peaceful surroundings, despite her minimal income and occasional recurrences of intestinal problems and a "tropical fluke" picked up in Honduras.

In 1952, Hurston served as a reporter for *The Pittsburgh Courier* on the sensational trial of Ruby McCollum in Live Oak, Florida. Angered that the all-white jury had sentenced Ruby, a black woman, to death for the killing of her white lover, Hurston called in author William Bradford Huie to help overturn the sentence. McCollum was declared incompetent and committed to an asylum and Huie went on to write a book about the incident entitled *Ruby McCollum: Woman in the Suwanee Jail.* One chapter was penned by Zora Hurston. The entire event became something of a last hurrah for Hurston.

During the quiet years spent at Eau Gallie, she began writing an epic book about the Biblical character Herod the Great, an idea that had burned within her since her time in Honduras. She was sure it would interest movie producer Cecil B. De Mille and she even wrote Winston Churchill, asking him to write the introduction. No one, however, not even her publishers, was interested in the idea. When asked by Scribner's to cut and focus the material, she refused, saying she could not bear to cut out her extensive research.

Within a few years, her little house and the land around it where she'd grown her garden were sold, and she was forced to move out. The spring of 1956 found her traveling to Merritt Island, across the Indian

River from Cocoa, where she took a job as a librarian for the Pan American technical library at Patrick Air Force Base. In her position as a clerk, she was to organize and log technical literature, a boring job that she detested, and she was terminated in less than a year. The reason her supervisor gave was that Hurston was "too well educated for the job." (Hemenway, 346) The librarian position provided Hurston with unemployment benefits. The checks weren't large, but Hurston had learned to get by on very little. She found a house trailer near the Indian River and lived there for a time.

By the fall of 1957, Hurston was living in Fort Pierce and writing for the small weekly newspaper, the *Fort Pierce Chronicle*. C.E. Bolen, the owner of the paper who had invited her to come and write for him, noted that Hurston had never become accustomed to having a boss. "She was a writer and naturally, was pretty well set in her ways," Bolen said. "That would cause some opposition, but we got along okay." (Nathiri, 38–39)

For a time she worked as a substitute teacher at the all-black Lincoln Park Academy school, but again she was fired. In a letter to the Florida Department of Education dated March 7, 1958, she wrote, "My name as an author is too big to be tolerated, lest it gather to itself the 'glory' of the school here. I have met that before. But perhaps it is natural. The mediocre have no importance except through appointment. They feel invaded and defeated by the presence of creative folk among them." (Nathiri, 39)

Hurston was befriended by Marjorie Alder, a radio and newspaper journalist who, by her own admission, was a great fan of Hurston's writings. She enjoyed the times they spent together in Alder's riverfront home, where Hurston—now terribly overweight at nearly two hundred pounds—enjoyed dressing in exotic outfits complete with colorful turban and entertaining Alder's white guests.

At the time Alder and Hurston became acquainted, Hurston was living in a small, green, concrete-block house located on School Court Road in Fort Pierce that she rented from Dr. Clem C. Benton, a local physician, for $10 a month. When Alder became aware that Hurston was practically penniless, she petitioned Dr. Benton to allow Hurston to live in the house rent-free, something he was pleased to do.

As she had done with her little cabin in Eau Gallie, Hurston beautified the grounds with azaleas, morning glories, and gardenias in addition to growing a thriving vegetable garden. Her health continued to deteriorate as she suffered from gall bladder attacks, stomach and intestinal problems, arthritis, and high blood pressure. Her mind, however, was still sharp.

"She was always studying," Dr. Benton said of Hurston. "Her mind ... just worked all the time." The kindly doctor stopped by her house after he closed his office, sometimes bringing her groceries, and the two sat and visited for hours. "I considered it an honor to sit and listen at her experiences as a writer, how she could go in and analyze, her method of getting background." (Nathiri, 41)

Dr. Benton described how Hurston, ever resourceful, created a desk and bookshelves out of fruit crates. Even though she was no longer in contact with publishing houses, she continued to work at her typewriter almost daily.

Hurston's brother Clifford and his wife Mabel came to visit Hurston while she lived in Fort Pierce and offered to help put her in a better place, but she refused; her pride would not allow her to accept their assistance. In later years, some critics thought there was a rift in the family, but all Hurston's siblings and her nieces and nephews admired and loved her.

After Hurston's elder brother Bob (Dr. Robert Hurston) passed away in 1933, she allowed his two daughters to come and live with her for a time in Eatonville. Winifred Hurston Clark remembered those happy days: "She was really good to live with. She was interesting ... I remember what good fried fish she cooked, and cole slaw; I'll never forget that. I just enjoyed living with her."(Nathiri, 64)

Hurston was a wanderer and she didn't stay long in any one place; family members learned to expect her to visit unannounced, but that didn't mean they were estranged. Lucy Hurston-Hogan, daughter of Hurston's younger brother Everett, testified that her father adored Zora, and filled his apartment with memorabilia of his famous sister.

A year earlier Hurston had undergone a brief hospital stay, after which she was issued funds from the Department of Welfare to purchase medicine and food. On October 12, 1959, Hurston was admitted to Fort Pierce Memorial Hospital after suffering a stroke. Before the month was out she was well enough to be transferred to the segregated Lincoln Park Nursing Home, operated by the St. Lucie County Welfare Agency. At this time, Dr. Benton said her speech was impaired and she had lost much of her coordination. While she could still engage in conversation with the doctor, she was now unable to write. Her old clacking typewriter sat in silence for the first time in many years.

Hurston lingered for almost three months before her death on January 28, 1960.

EPILOGUE

No one knows for sure Hurston's age when she died, because no one knows the year of her birth. Mrs. Moseley, a lady from Eatonville who remembered Hurston from childhood, said the famous author was at least sixty-nine when she died. By Hurston's calculations—which varied from time to time—she would have been as young as fifty-two. That ambiguity was part and parcel of Hurston's personality. In her book *Their Eyes Were Watching God*, she has Janie say, "The worst thing Ah ever knowed her to do was taking a few years offa her age and dat ain't never harmed nobody." (Nathiri, 45)

Marjorie Alder, as a correspondent for the *Miami Herald*, wrote an article regarding the passing of the noted author Zora Neale Hurston, stating there was not enough money for the funeral. As a result, funds came in from some of Hurston's friends and her publishing houses. Of her family members, only Clifford and Mabel Hurston were present at the funeral. Hurston was buried in an unmarked grave in the Fort Pierce segregated cemetery, the Garden of the Heavenly Rest. In time, the place became overgrown with tall weeds, all but forgotten.

Had it not been for Marjorie Alder, even Hurston's remaining manuscripts might have been destroyed. When Hurston was taken to the nursing home, a large trunk full of her belongings accompanied her. After her death, when the trunk went unclaimed, it was to be burned. Learning about the trunk from neighbors, Alder contacted the county judge to appoint her guardian of the materials. When a black deputy named Patrick N. Duval arrived at the nursing home to pick up the trunk, it was already being burned. He put out the fire with an ordinary garden hose, thus saving many of Hurston's papers and keepsakes, including the manuscript of the Herod story. These papers—some with burned edges—were donated to the Department of Rare Books and Manuscripts at the University of Florida Library in Gainesville.

Zora Neale Hurston remained nearly forgotten until the early seventies, when author Alice Walker read *Their Eyes Were Watching God*.

That book and Hurston's style of writing so touched Alice that she made a trip to Eatonville to learn more about Hurston's life. While there, she located the neglected gravesite and purchased a headstone to be placed on it. Engraved on the stone are these words:

Zora Neale Hurston
"A Genius of the South"
1901–1960
Novelist, Folklorist
Anthropologist

Walker's article "Looking for Zora," published in *Ms.* magazine, helped to spread the word about Hurston and to rekindle interest in her work. In 1977, Alice Walker and the Feminist Press published *I Love Myself When I Am Laughing*, an anthology made up of some of Hurston's most famous works.

During this time, Robert E. Hemenway became interested in Hurston's life and set out on an eight-year journey to research and then write her biography. *Zora Neale Hurston: A Literary Biography* was published in 1977, giving the reading public one of the fairest and most objective views of Hurston ever written.

Since then, study of Hurston's works has experienced a revival in colleges and universities all across the nation. A collection of her works has been published by the Library of America, making her the first African-American to be so honored. In 1991, the Zora Neale Hurston Society was organized by founder Ruth Sheffey, a professor of English at Morgan State University in Baltimore, Maryland.

After a number of years, even Eatonville became aware of Hurston's place in literary history. In January 1990, the town held the first annual Zora Neale Hurston Festival of the Arts. Alice Walker was present for the event, as were many of Hurston's family members. During the festival the Association to Preserve the Eatonville Community, Inc. dedicated the Zora Neale Hurston Memorial in honor of their famous citizen. A festival has been held every year since, allowing thousands of people to visit the incorporated black community that produced the genius of Zora Neale Hurston.

Watching the festivities and seeing Hurston's name emblazoned all about the community, one could surmise that she is still, just as her mother instructed her, jumping "at de sun."

WORKS CITED

Bloom, Harold, ed. *Modern Critical Views: Zora Neale Hurston.* Philadelphia: Chelsea House Publishers,1986.

Hemenway, Robert E. *Zora Neale Hurston, A Literary Biography.* Chicago: University of Illinois Press, 1977.

Howard, Lillie, P. *Zora Neale Hurston.* Boston: Twayne Publishers, 1980.

Hurston, Zora Neale. *Dust Tracks on a Road.* New York: HarperCollins, 1991. Originally published by Lippincott in 1942.

Nathiri, N.Y, ed. *Zora Neale Hurston: A Woman and Her Community.* Orlando: Sentinel Communications Company, 1991.

Walker, Alice, ed. *I Love Myself When I Am Laughing.* New York: The Feminist Press, 1979.

Wall, Cheryl A. *Women of the Harlem Renaissance.* Indianapolis: Indiana University Press, 1995.

AMY SICKELS

Voices of Independence and Community: The Prose of Zora Neale Hurston

INTRODUCTION

For years unknown, forgotten, or simply ignored by literary scholarship, the work of Zora Neale Hurston has been resurrected and is now widely read, studied, and praised. Hurston's impressive body of work includes four novels, two books of folklore, an autobiography, and over fifty short stories, essays, and plays.

A key figure among the literati of the Harlem Renaissance, Hurston was popular during her time and her work was generally well-received by mainstream American reviewers, but several prominent African-American male authors criticized and dismissed her for not writing socially realistic novels documenting the urban black experience and white racism—the dominant style of the day. Hurston's early short stories and the novel she is best known for, *Their Eyes Were Watching God* (1937), characteristically embraced black folklore and rural culture.

Hurston was most productive during the Depression; she was one of the most widely acclaimed African-American authors between 1925 and 1945. By the 1950s, when her political views turned more conservative, Hurston had moved away from her most common themes and thus her creative inspiration, and her work disappeared into obscurity. Her last published novel, *Seraph on the Suwanee* (1948), is typically considered a disappointment, if not a failure.

Hurston struggled financially and at one point made her living as a housekeeper; she died in obscurity in 1960 while living in a county welfare home, and was buried in an unmarked grave at a segregated cemetery. Her work, including *Their Eyes Were Watching God*, which was out of print for nearly thirty years after its first publication, virtually disappeared.

A revival of Hurston's work in the seventies can be at least partially attributed to Alice Walker's seminal essay "The Search for Zora Neale Hurston," a chronicle of Walker's search for and then marking of Hurston's grave that was published in *Ms.* magazine in 1974. Now, nearly thirty years later, *Their Eyes Were Watching God* is a popular title on college syllabi, and Hurston's writing receives wide scholarship and academic attention.

Hurston's fiction, which had been derided by a few key critics for being quaint, now seems progressive and unique for its time. In works such as *Their Eyes Were Watching God*, Hurston dared to explore the life of an African-American woman reaching self-autonomy, challenging notions of individuality and community, and questioning sexism within African-American society. Hurston's exploration of rural Southern black communities and the rich voices of black folklore proudly affirms and embraces African-American culture.

THE HARLEM RENAISSANCE

In the 1920s and early 1930s, Harlem was a mecca for African-American artists, writers, intellectuals, and musicians; it served as the center for the New Negro Movement, later known as the Harlem Renaissance. This movement focused on establishing a new cultural identity, fighting against the white stereotypes of blacks and embracing autonomy. During a time when many Southern African-Americans had migrated to the North seeking employment, and the country was steeped in Jim Crow laws and racist ideologies, hope for the future and belief in the need for changes was reflected in the arts.

Between 1919 and 1930 more African-American authors were published in greater numbers than during any other decade in America prior to the 1960s. Scholar and critic Alain Locke, also an early friend of Hurston's, was one of the main proponents of the New Negro Movement, urging young writers to "speak for the masses by expressing the race spirit" (Hemenway, 41). He encouraged artists to utilize their folk background and African heritage in the creation of their art, with the future promising progress.

The Harlem Renaissance occurred during America's Jazz Age; while Harlem was a vibrant center for African-American arts, culture, and politics, Harlem's speakeasies and jazz clubs became fashionable places for whites to gather. Whites were drawn to Harlem for its "primitive" and "exotic" aspect, and often attended parties and social functions, only to return to their white neighborhoods by the next morning. During this time many African-American artists, including Hurston, were funded by white patrons.

Although Hurston actually only resided in Harlem for two years, her influence on and association with the Harlem Renaissance is legendary. Robert Hemenway explains in his biography of Hurston that, despite disputes about Hurston's conservative political views in her later years and her controversial statements about such topics as segregation and Jim Crow, she was a "dedicated Harlem Renaissance artist," and through her writing she hoped to "transfer the life of the people, the folk ethos, into the accepted modes of formalized fiction." (Hemenway, 56)

Arriving in New York in 1925, Hurston wrote several short stories and plays in the twenties and organized the literary magazine *Fire!*, a journal devoted to younger Harlem artists, with Langston Hughes and Wallace Thurman in 1926. Although the editors only published one issue, Hurston's involvement demonstrates the active role Hurston played within the African-American artistic community. Her relationship with some of these artists, though, was somewhat tenuous, as demonstrated in 1931, when close friends Hurston and Hughes fought over *Mule Bone*, a play they co-created.

Hurston's first book was not published until 1934. Her Southern background and the focus of her writing differed from many of her contemporaries and critics, including Richard Wright and Alain Locke, who were invested in the style of social realism and naturalism popular in the thirties. Writers hoped to depict "real" African-American life, debunking racist stereotypes by embracing community values, political ideology, and a positive self-image. Hurston's work did not fall neatly into this category; her writing, rich with lyrical prose and folkloric symbols, focused on a small community of African-Americans in the South and their relationships with each other, without overtly addressing society's widespread racism. With her strong, independent

female characters and her focus on relationships between African
Americans instead of confrontations between African Americans and
whites, it is not surprising that Hurston was criticized. Few other writers
were charting the psychological independence of African-American
women, nor were writers focusing on rural Southern African-American
communities.

BLACK FOLKLORE

Hurston—flamboyant, outspoken, and independent—was a Southerner,
and even while living in New York, she wrote about the rural South,
embracing its folklore and the small town traditions of storytelling. She
was known on the New York scene for her comical and outrageous
"Eatonville" stories, which she liked to tell at parties and gatherings. As
Hurston succinctly states in her autobiography, "I was a Southerner, and
had the map of Dixie on my tongue."

Hurston first began collecting folklore after enrolling at Barnard
College in 1925 to study anthropology under the renowned
anthropologist Frank Boas. Hurston was thirty-four years old when she
enrolled, but throughout her life she claimed to be ten years younger,
passing herself off as a woman in her twenties during the time of the
New Negro Movement, when strong emphasis was placed on the youth
of the artists. Hurston made her first anthropological trip to Florida in
1927; nearly a year later, funded by her patron Charlotte Mason,
Hurston returned to Florida to collect black folklore, and much of this
productive field work appeared in her book *Mules and Men* (1932), the
first book of black folklore collected by an African American. Immersing
herself in the culture of several rural Southern African-American
communities, she recorded stories, songs, sermons, proverbs, superstitions, and folktales while actively participating in the communities.

Folklore, usually defined as the traditional beliefs and legends of a
people, especially when formed as part of an oral tradition, had been a
part of Hurston's life since childhood. "I was glad when somebody told
me, 'You may go and collect Negro folklore'," she wrote. "In a way it
would not be a new experience for me. When I pitched headforemost
into the world I landed in the crib of negroism. From the earliest rocking
of my cradle, I had known about the capers Brer Rabbit is apt to cut and
what the Squinch Owl says from the house top." Still, she needed "the

spy-glass of Anthropology" to distance herself from this culture, so that she could fully see its richness and layers. In "Zora Neale Hurston's Traveling Blues," Critic Cheryl Wall states, "The cultural relativity of anthropology freed Hurston from the need to defend her subjects' alleged inferiority."

Hurston was attracted to folklore because she could see that African Americans "were creating an art that did not need the sanction of 'culture' to affirm its beauty" (Hemenway, 54), and anthropology offered her a scientific way to record the cultural and intellectual richness of this art form. When one of the Eatonville residents asked, "Who you reckon want to read all them old-time tales about Brer Rabbit and Brer Bear?" Hurston replied that an audience did indeed exist and that she wanted to record the tales before "everybody forgets all of 'em." Hurston understood the importance of preserving the tales, and anthropology provided a structure for recording the folklore, "a pattern of meaning for material that white racism consistently distorted into stereotypes." (Hemenway, 215) Her work as an anthropologist and as a creative writer clearly overlapped; the folklore she collected fueled her fiction and provided her with a unique perspective and original material.

In spite of her training as an anthropologist, Hurston was never a conventional scientist, as demonstrated in the untraditional narrative structure of *Mules and Men*, an intimate portrait of African-American communities in the South, and Hurston's own connection to these communities. Brimming with folktales, songs, sermons, hoodoo, jokes, and tall tales or "lies," *Mules and Men* celebrates rural African-American folklore, and it is the first of several of Hurston's books to explore this theme.

Some of the most lively sections in both *Mules and Men* and her autobiography, *Dust Tracks on a Road*, concern Polk County, a sawmill and railroad town near the Everglades "where they really lies up a mess and dats where dey make up all de songs and things lak dat." In these works, she collects tales about "Ole Massa" and John, the slave who outwits him, and records the local folk songs, thereby capturing the spirit and attitudes of the place: "Polk County. After dark, the jooks. Songs are born out of feelings with an old beat-up piano, or a guitar for a mid-wife. Love made and unmade. Who put out dat lie, it was supposed to last forever?" Hurston explores the roots of community, where "the impulse is not to isolate oneself, but to lose the self in the art and wisdom of the group." (Hemenway, 166) This theme would appear throughout her career, in her stories, plays, and novels.

Over the years Hurston explored the hidden rural communities of Florida, New Orleans, and the Caribbean. *Tell My Horse*, a book of folklore based on her observations of voodoo in Haiti, was written three years after the publication of *Mules and Men*, but did not sell well; her biographer calls it her "poorest book," for the reason that Hurston was a "novelist and folklorist, not a political analyst or traveloguist." (Hemenway, 249).

On the other hand, *Mules and Men* succeeds because of its unique focus on not only Southern black communities but also Hurston's involvement with them. It is not a traditional anthropological report: rather than providing a detached, impersonal account of an "other" culture, Hurston depicts herself as a central character—the book opens with Hurston's trip back to her hometown, one of her earliest sources of folklore, and the humor, songs, chants, jokes, and sermons in *Mules and Men* document her own experiences as well as the community's.

BLACK COMMUNITIES

Hurston grew up in Eatonville, Florida, the first all-black town to be incorporated in America. Hurston described Eatonville as "a pure Negro" town, in which segregation was not an issue because only African-Americans lived in and ran the town. This area, rich with guava and orange trees, first gave Hurston her sense of self and also provided her with the inspiration for many stories and the characters that would appear in her fiction. Hurston blended her experiences in Eatonville and the subject of black folklore in her work in order to establish themes of African-American autonomy and culture.

Eatonville figures in much of her fiction and appears in Hurston's "Eatonville Anthology," a series of short stories published in the *Messenger* in 1926, and her first novel *Jonah's Gourd Vine* (1934). Both works demonstrate her ear for dialect and her attraction to black folklore. Based on the lives of her own parents, *Jonah's Gourd Vine* follows the life of John Pearson, a physically strong, well-liked, womanizing preacher who moves his family to this unusual town. When he first hears of Eatonville, John is awestruck at the idea of an African-American town:

'You mean uh whole town uh nothin' but colored folks?
Who bosses it, den?'
   'Dey bosses it deyself.'
   'You mean dey runnin' de town 'thout de white folks?'

Upon arrival in Eatonville, John's wife Lucy immediately feels
connected to the African-American town: "Lucy sniffed sweet air laden
with night-blooming jasmine and wished that she had been born in this
climate. She seemed to herself to be coming home. This was where she
was meant to be." For Hurston's characters, Eatonville is the land of
promise and opportunity.

   Eatonville's prominence in Hurston's work highlights her belief in
the power of African-American communities that are self-run, without
any dependence on social, cultural, political, and economic systems
dominated by whites. Therefore the focus of most of her fiction is on the
African-American townsfolk that populate such places as Eatonville,
rather than on racial tensions between African-Americans and whites.

   Three years after *Jonah's Gourd Vine* was published, Eatonville
reappeared in *Their Eyes Were Watching God*, Hurston's most
accomplished and widely read work. The townspeople, filled with wit
and wisdom, play an important role in the novel's setting and narrative.
Soon-to-be mayor Joe Starks glorifies the significance of the town: "But
when he heard all about 'em makin' a town all outa colored folks, he
knowed dat was de place he wanted to be. He had always wanted to be
a big voice, but de white folks had all de sayso where he came from and
everywhere else, exceptin' dis place data colored folks was buildin'
theirselves." Again, Hurston favored African-Americans sustaining and
governing themselves without interference from white society, but
reviewers often interpreted Hurston's lack of confrontation between
African-Americans and whites in her writing as proof that she was
ignoring racism.

   For example, *Mules and Men* received mostly positive reviews until
Sterling Brown criticized the book, claiming the stories "should be more
bitter," and saying that they did not reflect the harsh racism in America,
especially in the South. Brown's view represents the type of criticism
that followed Hurston throughout her career, and perhaps contributed
to her more conservative politics in the later part of her life.

   Hurston, fiercely independent, expressed resentment of what she
termed the "sobbing school of Negrohood" in her somewhat

controversial essay "How It Feels to Be Colored Me." She also did not write about tragic African-American characters. "Negroes were supposed to write about the Race Problem," she complains in her autobiography. "I was and am thoroughly sick of the subject. My interest lies in what makes a man or a woman do such-and-so, regardless of his color." But Hurston could give contradictory viewpoints or express brash sentiments about race, as demonstrated in the same essay, when she dismisses slavery as "the price I paid for civilization."

In their dismissal of Hurston's politics, many critics wrongly simplified her fiction, often ignoring the progressive nature of her focus on African-American communities and strong African-American female characters. In reviewing *Their Eyes Were Watching God*, author Richard Wright claimed the novel was not "serious fiction," and that Hurston's novel followed in the tradition of "the minstrel technique that makes the 'white folks' laugh," and Alain Locke wondered when Hurston would "come to grips with motive fiction and social document fiction." Hurston shot back that Wright's work was not an African-American novel but "a treatise on sociology."

Hurston's views of race can be attributed to her strong belief in individuality. Henry Louis Gates Jr. explains in his afterword to *Their Eyes Were Watching God* that Hurston railed against "the idea that racism has reduced black people to mere ciphers, to beings who only react to an omnipresent racial oppression."

Though her comments on racism in her fiction are often subtle, she certainly did not ignore the subject. For example, in *Their Eyes Were Watching God*, after a hurricane destroys the town, the white officials order that the white corpses be buried in coffins, while the African-American corpses be left to rot: "And don't lemme ketch none uh y'all dumpin' white folks, and don't be wastin' no boxes on colored." Furthermore, Hurston often spoke to the complexities of racism within the African-American community. For example, Mrs. Turner, an African-American character in *Their Eyes Were Watching God*, only befriends Janie because she is mulatto, claiming, "We oughta lighten up de race." While Hurston's main focus did not concern the racism of society, she did not belittle the subject.

Hurston's fiction portrayed African-American culture without defining it in relation to dominant white culture. She "asserted that black people, while living in a racist society that denied their humanity, had created an alternative culture that validated their worth as human beings."(Wall, 77) By writing of viable working-class African-American communities that were financially and culturally independent of whites, Hurston put forth her view that African-Americans could rise above the racist society by creating their own communities, not by imitating or hoping to "rise" to white society. Far from "quaint," Hurston's folklore and fiction is poignant in its portrayal of the "common people" who were not concerned with moving up into the white world, but were creating their own art and poetry and stories from the depths of their own heritage.

THE POETRY AND SYMBOLISM OF HURSTON'S LANGUAGE

The richness and layers in black folklore influenced nearly all of Hurston's writing, not only in terms of subject but also style. For example, Hurston has been criticized for making up parts of her life and deleting other parts in her autobiography, but this is the exaggerated and hyperbolic style of folktales and "lies" that makes it unique. Hurston claims a hog taught her how to take her first steps: "They tell me that an old sow-hog taught me how to walk. That is, she didn't instruct me in detail, but she convinced me that I really ought to try." It is when her writing displays such playfulness that Hurston's work feels the most intimate. The style of her best writing showcases metaphors, imagery, and allegories that draw the reader into a rich, vibrant world; it is the kind of language Hurston claimed was part of the African-American tradition, the "will to adorn." By both writing about this mode of language and using it herself in her writing, she was continuing the tradition.

Because Hurston brought black folklore and rhetorical styles into her fiction, her work embraced lyric symbolism and rhythmic diction. Her first novel, *Jonah's Gourd Vine*, provides Hurston with a space in which to depict folklore and African-American expression. The characters often speak in idioms, such as "A'll give mah case to Miss Bush and let Mother Green stand mah bond" or "God don't eat okra." Hurston also includes full-length passages of John's sermons as a way to represent the poetry of the preacher. Although there are many admirable aspects of the novel, it is often criticized for its undeveloped characters and the pages of folklore that sometimes overwhelm the

narrative. The Southern diction at times feels forced within the
narrative, reflecting the tension between Hurston's dual identities of
anthropologist and novelist.

Hurston mastered this style three years later in *Their Eyes Were
Watching God*, which she wrote in Haiti in only seven weeks, feeling as
though the story "was dammed up in me, and I wrote it under internal
pressure." The fictional romance with Tea Cake was based on Hurston's
true life romance with a Columbia student; as she explains, "The plot
was far from the circumstances, but I tried to embalm all the tenderness
of my passion for him." Her language captures the range of spoken
African-American voices—the witticisms, stories, jokes—within the text.
Henry Louis Gates Jr. calls this novel an example of the "speakerly text,"
a written work that represents an oral literary tradition. Using this
innovative style, Hurston could "represent various traditional modes of
Afro-American rhetorical plots while simultaneously representing her
protagonists' growth in self-consciousness through free indirect
discourse." (Gates, 175)

The novel opens with a distant third person narrator, speaking in
a storyteller voice, who sets up the novel's story-within-a-story structure
by describing the heroine Janie Crawford as a woman who "had come
back from burying the dead." The narrative then moves into the
dialogue between Janie and her friend Pheoby with "Pheoby's hungry
listening helped Janie to tell her story." The idea that the reader is
"overhearing" Janie's story prevails, even though the story is not
presented in first person but in a third person narrative voice that
embodies the rich, intimate African-American dialect. Unlike Hurston's
first novel, *Their Eyes Were Watching God* uses this narrative technique to
advance the plot and develop memorable and moving characters.

Hurston's language moves effortlessly from a third person
narrative voice to the dialectical, metaphor-rich language of the
characters, and through these fluid shifts of language, Gates claims
Hurston has found a third term, or a new way of telling. He describes
the two narrative poles as the African-American oral tradition and the
standard English literary tradition and states that "The quandary for the
writer was to find a third term, a bold and novel signifier, informed by
these two related yet distinct literary languages. This is what Hurston
tried to do in *Their Eyes*." (Gates, 158). There are places in the text in
which the narrative voice blends standard English and African-American

dialect, portraying the world through Janie's eyes. When the men are at the store telling "lies," the narrative interrupts their dialogue: "But here come Bootsie, and Teadi and Big 'oman down the street making out they are pretty by the way they walk. They have got that fresh, new taste about them like young mustard greens in the spring, and the young men on the porch are just bound to tell them about it and buy them some treats."

Hurston does not focus solely on Janie, but expands the narrative scope to include the stories of minor characters, namely the men who sit and tell stories on the porch of Joe Starks's store. The play of African-American language, the "lies," and the idea of rhetorically showing off or "signifying," is best demonstrated here; these stories-within-stories exhibit the play of double-speak, intricate metaphors, and tropes of vernacular African-American language. The porch is also an important symbol of Hurston's childhood, the place that was "the heart and spring of the town."

Gates notes that the novel's narrative is presented "through several subtexts or embedded narratives presented as the characters' discourse, of traditional black rhetorical games or rituals. It is the text's imitation of these examples of traditionally black rhetorical rituals and modes of storytelling that allows us to think of it as a speakerly text." (Gates, 178) The characters on the store porch often try to outdo each other in the colorfulness and exaggeration of their stories, performing the language for each other.

Hurston provides an example of the way she learned to speak in her autobiography, claiming that Southern children are "raised on simile and invective. They know how to call names ... They can tell you in simile exactly how you walk and smell. They can furnish a picture gallery of your ancestors, and a notion of what your children will be like. What ought to happen to you is full of images and flavor." This image-laden prose brings vibrancy to her words and intimacy to her descriptions. For example, when describing the death of her mother in *Dust Tracks on a Road*, she writes: "The Master-Maker in His making had made Old Death. Made him with big, soft feet and square toes. Made him with a face that reflects the face of all things, but neither changes itself, nor is mirrored anywhere." In describing her family's poverty she writes: "There is something about poverty that smells like death. Dead dreams dropping off the heart like leaves in a dry season and rotting around the feet ... People can be slave-ships in shoes."

In the article "Characteristics of Negro Expression" Hurston describes the African-American way of speech as using "action words," providing examples such as "'chop-axe,' 'sitting-chair,' 'cook-pot' and the like" and she continues to explain the concept: "Everything illustrated. So we can say the white man thinks in a written language and the Negro thinks in hieroglyphics." She expresses this idea in *Their Eyes Were Watching God*: "When the people sat around on the porch and passed around the pictures of their thoughts for the others to look at and see, it was nice. The fact that the thought pictures were always crayon enlargements of life made it even nicer to listen to."

This picture style of language appears not only in Hurston's lyricism and in her characters' dialogue, but also in the symbolism of her work. A train, embodying movement, power, and male sexuality, is described as a "panting monster," frightening and impressing John Pearson when he first sees it in *Jonah's Gourd Vine*. Later, he does not want to go back to live with his family on the other side of the creek but wants to live "where the train came puffing into the depot twice a day." Ironically, in the end it is the train that kills John.

Hurston's mastery of her symbolic language is most evident in *Their Eyes Were Watching God*. A repeating image, one that also appears in her autobiography, is a tree, specifically a flowering pear tree. The tree first appears at the moment of Janie's sexual awakening, a moment when Janie is inside herself and understands what she wants: "She was stretched out on her back beneath the pear tree soaking in the alto chant of the visiting bees, the gold of the sun and the panting breath of the breeze when the inaudible voice of it all came to her." This is the moment when Janie believes she has reached her full "conscious life." Her grandmother, who forces her to marry Logan Killicks, represents what Janie does not want to become: "Nanny's head and face looked like the standing roots of some old tree that had been torn away by storm" and the "vision of Logan Killicks was desecrating the pear tree." Many years later, after two unsuccessful and oppressive marriages, Janie falls in love with Tea Cake, and here the image of the flowering pear tree returns: "He could be a bee to a blossom—a pear tree blossom in the spring."

Similarly, in an early short story, "Sweat," Delia, enduring the abuse and torment of her husband, realizes that love has disappeared from their marriage, understanding that "[a]nything like flowers had long ago been drowned in the salty stream that had been pressed from her heart" and she finds the only peace in her life is her home: "She had built it for her old days, and planted one by one the trees and flowers there. It was lovely to her, lovely."

AUTONOMY AND VOICE: A WOMAN'S SEARCH

Their Eyes Were Watching God is not only noteworthy for its language, but also for the strength of its protagonist, a black woman who reaches empowerment and self-autonomy. The African-American and feminist movements incited the renaissance of Hurston, and *Their Eyes Were Watching God* is often taught as a feminist text, a story about a woman's search for identity and self-reliance.

Janie Crawford, the heroine of the novel, is a fully realized character who discovers her independence through language and through the intimate relationships with the people in her life. After Janie discovers her sexuality under the pear tree, Nanny attempts to thwart what she considers a vulnerability, and she forces Janie to marry the old man Logan Killicks. In Nanny's eyes, Killicks, a property owner, will provide Janie with protection and material goods. Nanny, who was born under slavery, believes "De nigger woman is de mule uh de world so fur as Ah can see." When Joe Starks comes along, he offers Janie an escape and lures her with tales of an all-black town. Although Janie hesitates ("Janie pulled back a long time because he did not represent sun-up and pollen and blooming trees"), she decides to flee with Starks: "A feeling of sudden newness and change came over her."

Starks soon becomes the store owner and mayor of Eatonville, creating roads, adding lamp posts, and living in a house so large, "the rest of the town looked like servants' quarters," an image that likens Starks's power over the town and Janie to that of a slave owner. Starks flexes his power early in the novel when the townspeople ask Janie to provide words of encouragement about her husband the mayor. Starks interrupts with, "Mah wife don't know nothin' 'bout no speech-makin'. Ah never married her for nothin' lak dat. She's us woman and her place is in de home." Janie would like to indulge in the story telling, but Starks has forbidden her to participate, even though the other men consider Janie "uh born orator ... Us never knowed dat befo'. She put jus' de right words tuh our thoughts."

In a culture steeped in oral tradition, Joe has silenced Janie; she is a listener, not a participant. Starks insists that the store porch, colored with its stories and tales, remain a male-gendered space and thereby suppresses Janie's subjectivity. Janie immediately realizes what he has taken from her: "Joe spoke out without giving her a chance to say anything one way or another that took the bloom off of things ... she went down the road behind him that night feeling cold." Starks' favorite expression is "I god," a constant reminder of the almighty position he sees himself occupying.

The ability to manipulate language is a constant theme in Hurston's work. For example, in the later novel *Moses, Man of the Mountain*, God, often referred to as "the Voice," speaks to the hero Moses, providing this man with a "stammering tongue" that grants him the power to lead the people. Similarly, John Pearson in *Jonah's Gourd Vine* finds his power in voice through preaching, his words able to move and motivate the people. When John realizes that he can preach the word upon finding his voice, his language becomes more poetic and charged. He hears himself pray and exclaims: "If mah voice sound *dat* good de first time Ah ever prayed in de church house, it sho won't be de las."

John may be the man of words, but it is his wife Lucy who is the voice of truth. Although she has no platform from which to speak, as he does, her words are used to cut through his masculinity. When John tests her, asking her if she wished she had married a richer man, she answers, "If you tired uh me, ju' leave me. Another man over de fence waitin fuh yo' job." Her words threaten John, and he in turn threatens "tuh kill yuh jes' ez sho ez gun is iron." Lucy is the voice of encouragement and belief in John, but he refuses to listen, thus disempowering her.

Hurston shows speaking as something usually relegated to men. In her autobiography, she depicts the porch as a gathering place for men, though she often lingers to hear them talk. One of the only women who participates is Big Sweet of Polk County, who appears in *Mules and Men* and *Dust Tracks on a Road*, a woman who clearly inspired Hurston with her strength, independence, and her keen ability to manipulate language. When Hurston first comes into contact with Big Sweet, she is "specifyin'" or rhetorically showing off.

Wall emphasizes the importance of this character: "It was Big Sweet's talk though that first captured Hurston's attention. Her words were emblematic of her power, for they signaled her ownership of self ... Hurston believed that individual black women could base their personal autonomy on communal traditions. In doing so, her characters achieved their status as heroines." (Wall, 83–84) Big Sweet enters the male-dominated space through her voice, and eventually Janie will follow in this direction.

Although many of the male characters are big talkers, they are also lacking an understanding of their selves, of the interior, such as John Pearson in *Jonah's Gourd Vine*, who seems mystified at the way his life has turned out. Similarly, for Joe Starks, language is only a game or power play, while Janie reaches an understanding of the self, in part by learning the power of voice—both by speaking and by resisting speech.

After Joe berates her in the store, she "pressed her teeth together and learned to hush." She divorces herself psychologically from him: "She was saving up feelings for some man she had never seen. She had an inside and an outside now and suddenly she knew how not to mix them." She waits until Starks has grown old and then she speaks back to him in the store, in a significant scene that, Gates argues, rhetorically "kills" Starks. After Joe insults her, she "took the middle of the floor to talk right into Jody's face, and that was something that hadn't been done before." She tells Starks: "You big-bellies around here and put out a lot of brag, but 'tain't nothin' to it but yo big voice. Humph! Talkin' 'bout *me* lookin' old! When you pull down yo' britches, you look lak de change uh life." This scene depicts the power Janie has won through words: "Janie had robbed him of his illusion of irresistible maleness that all men cherish, which was terrible."

Following this scene, Joe becomes sick with kidney failure and finally dies, and Janie discovers freedom. Thus, Janie's use of her voice begins to lead her on the trail of self-discovery. This scene echoes the moment in "Sweat" when Delia, fed up with Syke's insults, finally stands up to him and speaks the truth: "Ah hates you tuh de same degree dat Ah useter love yuh ... Ah hates yuh lak uh suck-egg dog."

In Hurston's work, voice is important not only as a means of power, but as a way to carry on memories and stories. Memory affected Hurston's ventures into anthropology and fiction, with her memories of Joe Clark's store and the folktales that inspired her throughout her career. As an anthropologist, she had the opportunity to preserve the culture that had always been dear to her. In her writing, the alliance of memory and voice often concerns the relationships of women.

When Hurston's mother dies, she realizes her mother, "depended on me for a voice" (Hurston, 65). Her mother impacted Hurston's individuality and creativity, urging her daughter to "jump at de sun," and Hurston hoped to recapture her mother's life in her first novel. Thus, on her deathbed, Lucy reveals the secret of happiness to her daughter: "Don't you love nobody better'n you do yo'self," the advice moving from mother to daughter, contained in a female sphere.

Significantly, the opening of *Their Eyes Were Watching God* suggests "women forget all those things they don't want to remember, and remember everything they don't want to forget. The dream is the truth. Then they act and do things accordingly." The narrative operates on the structure of Janie *telling* her story to her friend Pheoby, claiming "muh mouf is in my friend's mouf." Unlike the men on the porch who try to outdo each other's "lies," constantly interrupting and arguing with each other, Janie and Pheoby have a dialogue based on truth-telling and true listening. By the end of Janie's tale and tale-within-tales, Pheoby has been changed: "Ah done growed ten feet higher from jus' listenin' tuh you, Janie." So that not only has Janie reached self-autonomy, but Pheoby, just by listening, has been affected, and perhaps has a better realization of love and what it means to be a woman.

When Janie meets Vergible (Tea Cake) Woods, who, unlike her first two husbands, Killicks and Starks, has no possessions or wealth, he invites her to play a game of checkers with him, something that Starks had never allowed, and Janie "found herself glowing inside. Somebody wanted her to play. Somebody though it natural for her to play." Tea Cake with all his charm and playfulness represents a chance for equality between men and women, and although their relationship does not fully reach this balance, it is certainly the fullest, most loving relationship for Janie. Not only does she come to realize that love "is lak de sea. It's uh movin' thing, but still and all, it takes its shape from de shore it meets, and it's different with every shore," Janie also progresses into independence. Tea Cake asks Janie if she wants to "partake wid everything," and she says she does, and when they go to work on the farms in the Everglades, "the muck," they share household chores and spend their nights with the community, singing, dancing, and telling stories. Here, unlike Joe Starks' store, Janie has found a voice: "Only here, she could listen and laugh and even talk some herself if she wanted to. She got so she could tell big stories herself from listening to the rest."

After Tea Cake is bitten by a rabid dog and, crazed, tries to kill Janie, she shoots him in self-defense. Afterward, Janie is ostracized by her peers, namely the men in the community, but she is strong enough to withstand their criticisms, and returns, filled with mourning, to Eatonville, where she finds a place for herself in the world—as an independent woman. She has reached the point of understanding where she will not live the way her grandmother expected, but her own way. She has shown that African-American women are not the "mules" of the world. Nanny "had taken the biggest thing God ever made, the horizon ... and pinched it in to such a little bit of a thing that she could tie it around her granddaughter's neck tight enough to choke her," but Janie realizes the fullness and opportunity of the horizon, and she "had found the jewel down inside herself."

By the end of the novel she realizes her love for Tea Cake has not died, and that his "memory made pictures of love and light against the wall. Here was peace." Thus, Janie understands her autonomous and fully conscious self, and the spirit of the Eatonville community is as important to the novel as Janie's self-discoveries. Wall posits that Hurston "asserted that black people, while living in a racist society that denied their humanity, had created an alternative culture that validated their worth as human beings. Although that culture was in some respects sexist, black women, like black men, attained personal identity not by transcending the culture but by embracing it." (Wall, 77)

While Hurston charted an African-American woman's journey toward autonomy in *Their Eyes Were Watching God*, most of the other Harlem Renaissance writers were documenting the stories of male protagonists; thus, Hurston dismantled and critiqued the very aspects of African-American male culture that others were working so hard to uphold. Now, *Their Eyes Were Watching God* is celebrated by critics as a feminist and African-American text. "Hurston was not the first Afro-American woman to publish a novel, but she was the first to create language and imagery that reflected the reality of black women's lives," asserts Wall.

Hurston's affirmation of African-American women and African-American culture has influenced such contemporary writers as Alice Walker, Toni Cade Bambara, and Gloria Naylor. In her foreword to Hemenway's biography, Walker opens with the line, "I became aware of my need of Zora Neale Hurston's work some time before I knew her work existed," exemplifying the importance of Hurston's writing. Examples of strong female characters can be found in Hurston's other texts, but it is clearly the novel that best withstands scrutiny.

POLITICS

Hurston's next novel, *Moses, Man of the Mountain* (1939), blends the biblical story of Moses leading the Hebrews out of Egypt with African-American folklore, and although critics consider this to be a highly ambitious novel, perhaps Hurston's most ambitious, the novel has not received the same scholarly focus, namely because the book fails in the respect that "its author could not maintain the fusion of black creative style, biblical tone, ethnic humor, and legendary reference that periodically appears." (Hemenway, 270) While the novel often draws on previous themes of the power of language, identity, and African-American folklore, it takes place in Egypt rather than the rural South.

The novel retells the story of Moses, with his "true" identity, that of Egyptian or Hebrew, never fully revealed. Instead Hurston focuses on the legends and myth-making stories that help to develop Moses, and then follows his own personal quest for identity as the leader of a people and a chosen man who can speak directly with God. As in her other work, Hurston explores African-American folklore, drawing on her anthropological research, and portrays Moses as a powerful hoodoo man.

Interestingly, when Moses, who is raised in the high court of Egypt, departs to Midean, he learns "the dialect of [the] people," and his power as a man of nature and hoodoo begins to evolve. He begins to speak in the rural black dialect reminiscent of Hurston's Eatonville cast, to "reinforce Moses' human qualities," and his vivid speech resembles the poetry of preacher John Pearson. The black dialect supplants the traditional rhetoric of the Bible, and although the tone is not always consistent, this unique element provides an example of one of the ways in which the novel addresses race.

In this novel, Hurston embarks on more politically influenced themes. With the differing views on Moses's "true" birthright, Hurston alludes to the idea of passing, and in one particularly moving passage, after Moses has left Egypt, she writes of this change: "Moses had crossed over. He was not in Egypt. He had crossed over and now he was not an Egyptian. He had crossed over."

The novel is a blend of serious and comic tone; Hurston satirizes both the bickering that goes on among the leaders and the slaves' reluctance to follow Moses, the latter serving as a commentary on the transition from slavery to freedom for black Americans. Thus, the novel is not a satire, but a serious exploration of emancipation, depicting the complexities of reaching freedom after years of bondage. Moses realizes "He had found out that no many may make another free. Freedom was something internal ... All you could do was to give the opportunity for freedom and the man himself must make his own emancipation."

Although Hurston focuses on freedom, in many ways this freedom is relegated only to men. Unlike *Their Eyes Were Watching God*, women are secondary characters in this novel, without voice or individuality. Her next novel, *Seraph on the Suwanee*, published nine years later, focuses on a woman protagonist, but one who does not reach the kind of self-realization that Janie discovered.

During the interim between *Moses, Man of the Mountain* and *Seraph on the Suwanee*, Hurston published essays and her autobiography *Dust Tracks on a Road* (1942). The autobiography was her most commercially successful book, and Hemenway believes part of this success is because the book "did not offend whites." Hurston was often criticized for playing to white sympathies, and the complexity of this issue is most apparent in her autobiography, which Alice Walker calls the most "unfortunate" book that Hurston published. Often the book seems to evade truth, and some sections, such as the descriptions of her patrons or the white man who helped birth her, seem excessive in their attempt to depict the goodness of whites. However, in defense of Hurston, *Dust Tracks on a Road* was Hurston's most heavily edited book, and her publisher insisted that some of the more politically controversial sections be cut entirely.

Refuting criticism that the book is evasive, critic Deborah Platt calls the autobiography "a discourse of resistance" in which Hurston "constructs a mytho-narrative wherein the persona created transcends the oppressive conditions of society and holds power over self and world" (Platt, 9, 11). In other words, although the autobiography shies away from issues of racism in the South, often to a point of criticism, it is clear that these aspects of society must have penetrated Hurston's life in some way; she controls the narrative by choosing what to share with the reader, in order to again create this self-sustained African-American community.

"That which she chooses to reveal is the life of her imagination, as it sought to mold and interpret her environment," states Gates in the afterword. "That which she silences or deletes, similarly, is all that her readership would draw upon to delimit or pigeonhole her life as a synecdoche of 'the race problem,' an exceptional part standing for the debased whole." The freedom of imagination for Hurston appears thematically in much of her work, and her autobiography is not necessarily avoiding issues, but embracing the creativity of memory and imagination.

Perhaps one influence on the tone of Hurston's autobiography is the place and circumstances in which she wrote it—she wrote the book while living in California at the home of a wealthy white woman, Katherine Mershon; similar to her situation at the start of her career, Hurston was again dependent on white patronage. Clearly, Hurston's relationship with her patrons could affect her work.

The most significant period of funding occurred early in her career, when Mrs. Charlotte R. Osgood Mason, or "Godmother," as she instructed Hurston to call her, funded Hurston as she collected folklore. Hurston gave up much of her own power to Mason, who for a short time was also Langston Hughes' patron. During the five years Hurston was collecting folklore for *Mules and Men*, Mason forbid Hurston to publish, and everything she collected was considered Mason's property. Hurston devotes a short section of *Dust Tracks on a Road* to describing her relationship with her white patron, fawning over her generosity, but the astute reader can glimpse the power structure of this relationship as Mason instructs Hurston, "Keep silent. Does a child in the womb speak?" (Hurston, 144).

Critic Barbara Johnson notes, "Hurston's joyful and lucrative gatepost stance between black and white cultures was very much a part of her Harlem Renaissance persona and indeed was often deplored by fellow black artists." However, this kind of relationship was not restricted to Hurston; many of the African-American artists were funded by white patrons during the Harlem Renaissance. Hurston's financial dependency on Mason complicated Hurston's position as a creative writer, and clearly some of Hurston's best work was produced in the periods where she was *not* reliant on her patrons.

While she may have been grateful for funding, Hurston understood the position of the African-American artist. Her evocative essay "What White Publishers Won't Print" (1950), grasps the racism inherent in the publishing industry and in society: "I have been amazed by the Anglo-Saxon's lack of curiosity about the internal lives and emotions of the Negroes, and for that matter, any non-Anglo-Saxon peoples within our borders, above the class of unskilled labor."

Hurston was often targeted for intentionally appealing to a white audience. Langston Hughes, once a friend of Hurston, later wrote about her in his autobiography: "To many of her white friends, no doubt, she was a perfect 'darkie.'" However, such criticisms simplify and undercut Hurston's dedication to her African-American roots, and her clear and strong views on the racism in America. Her essays, "My Most Humiliating Jim Crow Experience" (1944), and "Crazy for this Democracy" (1945), lambast the Jim Crow laws, and call for their complete repeal. She writes that in America "no one of darker skin can ever be considered an equal" and asserts that she will "give my hand, my heart and my head to the total struggle."

In the fifties her views grew more conservative, with her fear of Communism and her distrust of liberal Northerners fueling her politics. Her statements during this period have overshadowed her more radical and progressive views. In a 1955 letter published in the *Orlando Sentinel*, she objected to the Supreme Court's desegregation decision, and this brought much warranted criticism against her. However, it must also be understood that Hurston, who had been raised in an all-black town, feared that all African-American institutions were to be integrated with whites so that the students could be "introduced" to a "higher" way of learning.

The criticism of Hurston catering to white audiences also arises with her next and final novel, *Seraph on the Suwanee* (1948). The book is considered a failure by most critics, despite receiving mostly good reviews and selling well at the time of publication, albeit mostly to whites. It is her only novel where the central characters are white. Arvay Henson Meserve's life is constructed through her marriage to Jim Meserve, a sexist and oppressive man similar to Joe Starks. However, Arvay never reaches the autonomy or independence that Janie does, possible because she is "not given a stature that will support the psychological burden she is asked to bear." (Hemenway, 310)

Although all of the central characters are white, they often speak like the characters of Eatonville, as if the African-American folklore can be erased of its culture, and so the dialogue seems out of context. Most critics agree that the main problem with this novel is that Hurston abandoned the source of her creativity, forsaking her love of African-American folklore and thus her creative inspiration.

In the last decade of her life, Hurston lived by herself in Florida and worked on a book about Herod the Great. Although during this time she had health problems and struggled financially, she was no longer dependent on patrons, and she was writing as much as she physically could.

The rediscovery of Hurston and her importance as an African-American, female writer has spawned her full revival, finally placing Hurston alongside other accomplished writers. With Hurston's anthropological field work in African-American folklore and her blend of Southern diction and poetic symbolism, she produced a unique, admirable oeuvre. Her characters succeed with their voices, overcoming dominating attitudes of sexism and racism in society; thus, Hurston's work uplifts the importance of female identity and independence, while also affirming and celebrating African-American culture.

Works Cited

Gates, Henry Louis, Jr. Afterword to *Their Eyes Were Watching God*, by Zora Neale Hurston. New York: Harper Perennial, 1990.

———, ed. *Zora Neale Hurston: Critical Perspectives Past and Present*. New York: Amistad, 1993.

———, ed. "Their Eyes Were Watching God: Hurston and the Speakerly Text." Gates 154–203.

Hemenway, Robert E. *Zora Neale Hurston: A Literary Biography*. Urbana and Chicago: University of Illinois Press, 1980.

Hurston, Zora Neale. "Characteristics of Negro Expression." *Negro: An Anthology*. Ed. Nancy Cunard. London: Negro University Press, 1969.

———. *Dust Tracks on a Road*. New York: Harper Perennial, 1996.

———. *Mules and Men*. New York: Harper Perennial, 1990.

———. *Zora Neale Hurston: Novels and Stories*. New York: The Library of America, 1995.

———. *Their Eyes Were Watching God*. New York: Harper Perennial, 1990.

Johnson, Barbara. "Thresholds of Difference: Structures of Address in Zora Neale Hurston." Gates 130–140.

Plant, Deborah G. "Metaphors of Self, Language, and the Will-to-Power." *Every Tub Must Sit on Its Own Bottom.* Urbana and Chicago: University of Illinois Press, 1995.

Wall, Cheryl A. "Zora Neale Hurston's Traveling Blues." *Women of the Harlem Renaissance.* Bloomington and Indianapolis: Indiana University Press, 1995.

———. "Zora Neale Hurston: Changing Her Own Words." Gates 76–97.

Walker, Alice, ed. *I Love Myself When I'm Laughing: A Zora Neale Hurston Reader.* New York: The Feminist Press, 1979.

———. Foreword to *Zora Neale Hurston: A Literary Biography,* by Robert E. Hemenway. Urbana and Chicago: University of Illinois Press, 1980.

ROBERT E. HEMENWAY

Crayon Enlargements of Life

Seeing Eatonville with a child's eyes meant that the harsh edges of life in a Jim Crow South seldom came into view. There was a willfulness about Hurston's celebration of her native village, and it eventually brought her criticism. The publication of *Mules and Men* in the fall of 1935 marked the start of an extended controversy over the nature and value of her work. Critics argued that a pastoral conception in *Mules and Men* distorted the reality of black life in America, a complaint that would follow her the rest of her career.

Zora had returned to New York in August, anticipating the book's publication in early October. Having very little money, she searched for employment among the various federal programs of the Works Progress Administration. By the time *Mules and Men* reached the bookstores, she had signed on as a "dramatic coach" at $23.86 per week on the WPA's Federal Theatre Project in New York.[1]

The immediate reception of *Mules and Men* was mixed. The nature of both the praise and the dissatisfaction came to characterize Hurston's public reputation for the next twenty years. Reviewers liked the book and recommended its lively stories. The *Saturday Review* called it "black magic and dark laughter," stressing the "entertainment" value. But Zora had not intended the book as light reading, and some reviewers accepted her invitation to a more serious interpretation. Written by a black

From *Zora Neale Hurston: A Literary Biography*. © 1977 by the Board of Trustees of the University of Illinois. Reprinted by permission.

author, about black people, it was assumed to reveal "what the Negro was really like," a subject of immense fascination to whites and of obvious vested interest to black readers. The *New York Times* reviewer wrote that Hurston encouraged the reader to "listen in" while "her own people" were being "natural," something they could never be in the company of outsiders. A white southerner, he felt assured that "at the end you have a very fair idea of how the other color enjoys life." Even Henry Lee Moon of the NAACP, reviewing the book in the *New Republic*, urged a larger meaning. Zora had not presented the life of the race as he lived it in New York City, but he was willing to assert that "*Mules and Men* is more than a collection of folklore. It is a valuable picture of the life of the unsophisticated Negro in small towns and backwoods of Florida."[2]

Discussed on this basis for a few months, the book finally drew the public attention of Sterling Brown. Brown was one of the best poets in America, the author of *Southern Road*, a book of poems inspired by folk sources. A graduate of Williams College, holder of a Harvard M.A., and a teacher at Howard, Brown had collected folklore in the South. Although he had not spent as much time in the field as Hurston, he knew well the dusty roads she had traveled. His review did not appear until February of 1936, but its thoughtful criticism was symptomatic of the kinds of questions many people—especially black, intellectuals—had begun to ask about Hurston's book.[3]

Brown stressed Zora's academic training and praised her rendering of the tales. He disliked some of the "sensationalism" in the hoodoo section, but on the whole found it worthy. He was less certain than Moon about the book's value as a portrait of black life. It was authentically done as far as it went, but the portrait of the South was incomplete; missing were the exploitation, the terrorism, the misery. Disputing Zora's claim that "the Negro storyteller is lacking in bitterness," Brown reported that he had often found expressions of anger and animosity. He objected to her "socially unconscious" characters, whose lives are "made to appear easy-going and carefree." Where was the smouldering resentment so often characteristic of the black South? He concluded, "*Mules and Men* should be more bitter; it would be nearer the total truth."[4]

Many black intellectuals believed that books by black authors needed to tell the "total truth" to white America. Books about the race should aim to destroy the absurd beliefs and racist fantasies of the suppressing culture, and such books would necessarily at times be bitter. But even if Hurston had consciously tried to avoid bitterness, Brown's criticism was important. She had not been writing for pure entertainment—although publisher's demands may have veered *Mules and Men* in that direction—and she had offered a portrait of the race meant to be taken as a behavioral example. Her preface promised access to the interior of the black mind, a report on what blacks deliberately kept from whites. But if this was her purpose, why had she excised the sharper edges, the harsher tones, of her rural informants? Nowhere in *Mules and Men* was there a discussion of the stories told in Eatonville of the Ocoee riot of November, 1920. Only a few miles away, in a scene well remembered by the community, black people had been denied their voting rights; when some protested, a white mob had burned and killed. One victim, July Perry, became legendary by defending his family and property, killing two white men before he was lynched and left swinging from a telephone pole beside the road to Eatonville.[5]

Published in the same year as the Scottsboro trial, *Mules and Men* has a disembodied quality about it, as if it came from a backwoods so far to the rear that American social history of the twentieth century had not touched its occupants. At a time when the Communist party was recruiting large numbers of black people, primarily because it was the only political party in America advocating an end to segregation, and when Richard Wright and Langston Hughes were creating a proletarian literature, Zora Hurston had deliberately chosen not to deal with the resentment of the black community. Why?

The reasons were strategic and philosophic, although she later admitted that publisher's restrictions also played a part. Hurston had a conception of the black image in the popular mind, and she felt that it derived largely from a mistaken notion of the black folk. The total truth was relative, making the class struggle seem less important than the need for an altered perception of black folklore; the Ocoee riot was not folklore, but history. Afraid of being thought "one of the sobbing school of Negrohood," Hurston was determined to prove that black people did not devote their lives to a morose discussion of white injustice. She once complained about the "false picture" created by black writers dwelling on the race problem, producing writing "saturated with our sorrows." This picture was false because it distorted: "We talk about the race problem a great deal, but go on living and laughing and striving like everybody else."[6] By leaving out "the problem," by emphasizing the art in the folkloric phenomenon, Hurston implicitly told whites: Contrary to your arrogant assumptions, you have not really affected us that much; we continue to practice our own culture, which as a matter of fact is more alive, more esthetically pleasing than your own; and it is not solely a product of defensive reactions to your actions. She felt that black culture manifested an independent esthetic system that could be discussed without constant reference to white oppression.

The price for this philosophy was an appearance of political naïveté and the absence of an immediate historical presence. *Mules and Men* really refers to an idealized Eatonville of Hurston's childhood memory. The town of the 1930s, hard hit by depression, seldom appears. Hurston privately acknowledged economic and racial realities, but the times called for a public indictment; her reticence offended those attacking racism by frontal assault. Zora's approach was oblique and open to misinterpretation. She chose to write of the positive effects of black experience because she did believe that white injustice had created a pathology in black behavior, a position brought into sharp focus in the criticism of her career by a white radical, Harold Preece.

One of the charges Zora had faced was common to all folklorists, but special to her because she was black. What was the collector's responsibility to the folk who provided the lore? Preece, in an article in the *Crisis* entitled "The Negro Folk Cult," saw a kind of professional colonialism in the way Hurston "was devoting her literary abilities to recording the legendary amours of terrapins," when she should be enlisted in the revolution; she should "cast her lot with the folk," rather than simply mine their traditions.[7]

Preece's politics were more radical than Hurston's, but politics did not constitute the primary difference between them. At the root of their argument was a contrasting conception of black folklore. Preece saw black traditions as basically evasive; and no matter what their intrinsic beauty, this evasive factor predominated. While this quality might be admirable for "protective purposes," he felt that it impeded further racial progress. Trickster figures like John, outwitting the master through cunning, were less a symbol of strength than the defensive creation of a psychologically captive and economically deprived people. Preece sympathized with those northern blacks who escaped the traditional culture, avoided the folklorist, and resented Zora Neale Hurston: "For when a Negro author describes her race with such a servile term as 'Mules and Men' critical members of the race must necessarily evaluate the author as a literary climber."[8]

Hurston's research convinced her that the intrinsic beauty of folk expression was by far its most important element. The protest impulse was not subordinated, but stylized so that it could survive. A kind of art grew from a phrase like "mules and men" because a collective esthetic impulse had transformed black people's identification with the mule—an overworked beast of burden—into a special symbol. The phrase meant not only that black people were treated as mules, but also that they were defiantly human—mules *and* men. The identification itself demonstrated how a negative relationship (slave : mule : beast of burden) could be transformed into a positive identity (beast of burden . mule . slave : man), with the content of the positive identification concealed from outside understanding. "Mules and men" was a phrase that *signified*—it had several meanings, many contexts.

From outside the race, a black person's identification with the mule was appropriate; it implied that one knew his place. From inside, the identification with the mule was only initially a recognition that one was being used as a beast of burden. Folklorist Alan Dundes has explained how the folkloric process sometimes operated with a reverse anthropomorphism, which noted the similarity between the mule's situation and that of the slave, then identified mulish traits with black people. Mules were bought and sold by massa just as slaves were. They were forced to work long hours just as slaves were. But the mule also represented admirable characteristics for a slave society: individualism, stubbornness, strength, and unpredictability. As Langston Hughes would later write, "I'm like that old mule ... Black / And don't give a damn! / So you got to take me / Like I am." Many stories and sayings about mules became allegories exhibiting the creative capacities of black storytellers defying their treatment as animals. The phrase "mules and men" never let one forget the perverse relationship with the master—it could simultaneously repudiate the unnatural servitude and affirm one's natural human condition. Put another way, Preece's objection to Hurston's title went straight to the question of whether black folklore resulted from the protective pathology of servility or the creative genius of survival.[9]

Folk art and behavior were inseparable to Hurston because she saw the creative impulse as the highest form of the black survival mechanism. She identified drama as a "characteristic" of black behavior, explaining the dynamics this way: "Who has not observed a young Negro chap posing up a street corner, possessed of nothing but his clothing, his strength and his youth? Does he bear himself like a pauper? No, Louis XIV could be no more in assurance.... His posture exults, 'Ah, Female.... Salute me, I am strength.' ... These little plays by strolling players are acted out daily in a dozen streets in a thousand cities, and no one ever mistakes the meaning."[10] The youth demonstrated the same sense of adornment that characterized black preachers and Eatonville storytellers: he was transforming his street-corner world into a stage. Hurston's emphasis was not on the economic system that seemed to make him a pauper, but on the drama that made him a king.

Hurston's critics of the thirties, concerned about the collapse of capitalism and its effects on black people, overlooked the implicit protest in her observations of this kind, and in much of her dramatic work as well. Zora joined the WPA Federal Theatre Project in the fall of 1935 not only because she sorely needed a job; she also still envisioned the stage as an appropriate vehicle for the affirmation of black lifestyles. Her celebratory manner confronted indirectly by asserting a positive view of black traditions. June Jordan has argued that this affirmative attitude is indeed an act of protest, given the American context.[11] Although not written specifically for the Federal Theatre Project, Zora's one-act play "The Fiery Chariot" illustrates her positive vision of the thirties. It attacks from an angle; yet its argument is forcefully direct, undercutting accepted interpretations about the origins of black Christianity while redefining the symbolism of good and evil.

In the notes to *Mules and Men* Zora observed that the devil in black folklore is not the terror he is in European folklore. Rather, he is a powerful trickster who often competes successfully with God. She added, "There is a strong suspicion that the devil is an extension of the story-makers while God is the supposedly impregnable white masters, who are nevertheless defeated by Negroes." This is a revolutionary principle, one which overturns the normative moral structure of the oppressing society. Bad becomes good, and vice versa, and this very perception protests the inadequacy of moral terminology in an oppressive culture. If God is a white man, the symbol of oppression, then white Christian claims to a God of love are dubious. Moreover, if the white man's power can easily be circumvented or defeated, often without punishment, the white man's God can hardly be a figure commanding instant, ungrudging obedience. The origin of the identification between black storyteller and devil trickster is almost impossible to discover and may even be an African survival. Its human logic is self-evident. Confronted with the hypocrisy and paradox of white Christianity's sanction of slavery, the slave might naturally identify with an opposing power. The linguistic effects of this identification, adapted through history, can be striking. When Sonia Sanchez titles a book of poems *We a BaddDDD People*, not only is she using black idiom, she is also reversing the vocabulary of moral dialogue by being true to the linguistic traditions of her race. Hurston's play "The Fiery Chariot" depends on this technique of ironic reversal. It illustrates how folklore can simultaneously affirm black life and protest white values.

Never published, "The Fiery Chariot" was first written in 1933 for inclusion in the Rollins performance of *From Sun to Sun*. Based on a widely known folktale Zora had collected in Florida, the action takes place on a plantation "before surrender." Ike is a tall black man, religiously inclined, who prays excessively each night for release from his life of toil and trouble: "Come Lawd, come in a good time and git yo humble servant and keer im to heben wid you. Come in yo' fiery chariot and take me way from dis sin-sick world. Massa work me so-ooo hard and Ah ain't got no rest nowhere." Tired of hearing this, Ole Massa decides to "see if he means what he prays," by dressing in a white sheet and knocking on Ike's door: "It's me, Ike, the Lord, I come in my fiery chariot to take you to heaven with me. Come right now, Ike." Going as slowly as possible to the door, Ike visibly starts when he sees the white being outside: "Oh, Lawd, you so white and clean, ah know you don't want me to go to heben wid you in dese ole dirty clothes. Gimme time to put on my Sunday shirt." After dressing, he asks the Lawd to step back from the door: "Oh, Lawd, the radiance of yo' countenance is so bright, ah can't come out by yuh." As he measures the distance between them, he gains more space: "Oh Lawd, heben is so high and ahm so humble in yo' sight, and yo' glory cloud is so bright and yo radiance is so compellment be so kind in yo' tender mercy as to stand back, jes' a little bit mo'." Ike then exits in great haste, calling out, "If thou be a running death, ketch me." His child ends the play by asking if his father will be caught and taken to heaven; the mother assures him that the Lawd cannot outrun his father, "and him barefooted too."[12]

At one level, "The Fiery Chariot" is an example of Massa making fun of a superstitious black slave. But if Ike is being tricked, he is also a trickster, and the play ultimately makes fun of a religion which posits heaven as an otherworldly surcease from a life of slavery on earth. At another level of consciousness, listeners to the tale or viewers of the play could not help noticing that, despite his apparent religion, Ike readily adapts to the reality of the situation; his instinct for survival transcends his spiritual faith, leading him to improvise an escape. The direction of the play shifts at the moment Ike realizes he will have to extricate himself from the consequences of his prayers.

The accepted white cliché about the origins of the black Christian church has always been that the notion of heaven was particularly appealing to laborers in bondage. While this life may be hard, if one trusted in the Lord a better day was coming over Jordan. But in "The Fiery Chariot" the Lawd is exposed as a fraud and a sham, nothing but a plantation owner masquerading in a sheet; the image becomes as ludicrous as that of the white man with a rack of antlers on his head in *Mules and Men*. The slave is made fun of, but so is Massa. He is soooooo bright, soooo "white and clean," and the black man is soooo humble in his sight that the Christian support for white supremacy is exaggerated into mockery. Ike becomes foolish in direct proportion to his belief in the bogus white God, wise in direct proportion to his ability to alter that belief in the interests of survival. The good Christian hoping for release would presumably go passively; but even Ike's wife recognizes the unnatural hope in his religious exercises: "Every night heah, down on yo' rusty knees beggin God to come git yuh and take you to heben in his fiery chariot. You know you don't want tuh die a bit more'n Ah do." Coincidentally, as the story passed through history, Ole Massa's foolish wearing of a sheet assumed an additional satiric content, the apparel of the Ku Klux Klan made to appear ridiculous. Moreover, as folklorist Gladys-Marie Fry has documented, the tradition of a night-riding ghost, dressed in a sheet, was one that whites had manipulated during both slavery and Reconstruction to attempt to intimidate, an intimidation comically exposed in Hurston's folk play.[13] In sum, the white sheet represents fraud, with no capability to clothe with either power or divinity.

"The Fiery Chariot" and *Mules and Men* illustrate important black creative styles, appearing on the surface to avoid protest, but, in Hurston's eyes, protesting profoundly by saying that this is the more beautiful, the more viable, the more human tradition. Zora informed whites that their values faded in comparison with black values, for black people were much better at making their lives a thing of beauty. This was a philosophy that had dominated her earlier essays in Cunard's *Negro*. Black religious services are an example of native esthetics distinguishing black and white Christianity: "Prayers and sermons are tooled and polished until they are true works of art.... The prayer of the white man is humorous in its bleakness." Black dancers move with an angularity that becomes "dynamic suggestion" and involves the spectator in the movement. In comparison with whites, "the Negro must be considered the greater artist." Blacks might imitate whites, not out of a feeling of inferiority, but for the love of the art itself. The measure of the black man's creativity is his adaptation of the source: "While he lives and moves within the midst of white civilization, everything he touches is reinterpreted for his own use." On the other hand, white attempts to imitate indigenous black expression prove only the absence of a creative soul: "God only knows what the world has suffered from the white damsels who try to sing Blues."[14] Zora once told a lecture audience that "white people are inclined to more restraint" because "they lack imagination."[15]

Hurston brought this pride in black esthetics to the Federal Theatre Project, where she played a prominent part in organizing the New York City division's special Harlem unit. Many talented black theater people were employees of the project, and the atmosphere was bright with hope. Zora helped with the Harlem unit's first production, *Walk Together Chillun*, and Elmer Rice, the project's director, announced in the *New York Times* that her untitled play would be among the forthcoming offerings. The play was probably untitled because it had been written in a week's time to secure the federal employment. As the haste might imply, Zora's interest in the theater project was short-lived. By April, 1936, when the Harlem unit staged its most famous production—*Macbeth*, directed by Orson Welles with an all-black cast and a setting in Napoleonic Haiti—Zora was in the West Indies herself, the recipient of a Guggenheim Fellowship. She proposed "to make an exhaustive study of Obeah (magic) practices ... to add to and compare

with what I have already collected in the United States." Zora accepted
the Guggenheim on March 18 and resigned her WPA job on March 20.
In less than a month she was in Jamaica, ready to begin a year of
intensive writing and collecting. As the Lafayette Theater reverberated
with the voodoo drumming Welles had imposed on Shakespeare,
Hurston sought out a living drama in the sound-filled nights of the
Caribbean.[16]

Zora arrived in Kingston on April 14. En route she had stopped for
a short time in Haiti, meeting a number of important government
officials and making preparations for her return in September. Ten days
later the Kingston *Daily Gleaner* ran a feature on the flamboyant visitor,
photographing her in jodhpurs and riding garb, her hat at a rakish angle,
ready for a sortie into the tropical bush. By the first week in May she had
already begun "to gather material wholesale." Leaving Kingston almost
immediately for the lush, green countryside, she had found that all she
had to do was make her collecting intentions known: "Just squat down
awhile and after that things begin to happen." She also made contacts
with the upper class and was struck by the intraracial color-
consciousness of the society and the sensitivity of the "coloureds," the
light-skinned elite: "I have corrected several who called me a *coloured*
person. They wonder why we insist on being called Negroes." Annoyed
at the tendency for mulattoes to speak only of their white male parent,
she thought of writing an article about "this island where roosters lay
eggs."[17]

This phrase became a chapter title in *Tell My Horse*, Zora's account
of her trip; together with her correspondence, the book becomes a kind
of diary for 1936–38. Her primary impression of Jamaica was of a
hopelessly chauvinistic, assimilationist culture. She asked if the search
for an ever-lighter race was the Jamaican answer to racial prejudice. If so,
then "perhaps we should strike our camps and make use of the cover of
night and execute a masterly retreat under white skins." Equally
offensive was the male domination in the society. She was told repeatedly
that "women who went in for careers were just so much wasted
material"; that "we men do not need your puny brains to settle the affairs
of the world"; that "wisdom-wise" western women should know that
"being a woman [sexually] is the only thing that you can do with any real
genius." The color-consciousness and the feminine oppression were
interrelated, she noted, for it was the dark-skinned black woman who

bore the brunt of both prejudices. If a woman was of no family, poor and black, "she had better pray to the Lord to turn her into a donkey and be done with the thing." She collected a bitter story of a young black girl, sexually used by her mulatto lover, then thrown away to preserve the "honor" of his marriage.

Zora had quickly learned about the treatment of women when she lost her letter of credit for the Guggenheim funds, along with $100 in cash, in a Kingston restaurant. The bank officials were condescending and uncooperative, and she worried that it meant the end to her fellowship. The experience was depressing not only because of the chauvinism of the police and the banking people, but also because it demonstrated her fiscal dependence: "I have no talents whatsoever in money and business matters.... I get too thoroughly immersed in my dreams. But somehow life is so organized that I find myself tied to money matters like a grazing horse to a stake."[18]

A new letter of credit was arranged, and the collecting continued. In late May she wrote Henry Allen Moe, director of the Guggenheim Foundation, that she had found a "gracious plenty," stressing that the Maroons of Jamaica "are worth a year's study in themselves." Descendants of men who fought their way out of slavery, the Maroons had resisted all subsequent attempts to reenslave them. One group, residing in the forbidding Saint Catharine Mountains at Accompong, represented exactly the kind of isolated community many folklorists hope to discover.[19]

Hurston spent much of her six months in Jamaica with these Maroons, living among them quietly. They offered to stage various dances for her benefit, but she declined: "I wanted to see their culture and art expressions and knew that if I asked for anything especially, I would get something out of context. I had heard a good deal about their primitive medicines and wanted to know about that. I was interested in vegetable poisons and their antidote. So I just sat around and waited."[20] The waiting eventually paid off: she was taken on a ritualistic hunt for a wild boar, and became friends with the chief medicine man of the tribe. A politically astute, ambitious man of extraordinary psychic power and herbal knowledge, he took her to a clearing on a hot summer afternoon and demonstrated his abilities. Using only the power of his mind, he willed to silence the thousands of croaking frogs of the nearby jungle. Although Zora did not learn how he did it, there was no questioning the effect. The sudden silence terrified.

This Maroon medicine Man revealed to Hurston that there was more to Jamaican folkways than the color-consciousness of the upper class and the chauvinism of the male elite. She concluded that "Jamaica is a seething Africa under its British exterior," and she began to explore the African survivals manifest in the native religion. By the middle of June she had enough raw data to begin to think about its organization:

> It has occurred to me to make a collection of all the subtle poisons that Negroes know how to locate among the bush and [in] the use of which they are so expert. No one outside the hoodoo or bush doctors know these things. But as I am learning day by day more and more I think that I will be doing medical science a great service to identify these weeds so that antidotes can be prepared. The greatest power of voodoo rests upon this knowledge. Some of these bushes are quite marvelous. One of them I *know* will kill by being placed so that the wind will blow from it to the victim. Another can be rubbed on the clothing and enters thru the pores as soon as the victim sweats.[21]

Hurston stayed in Jamaica until September 22, 1936, visiting all the island's parishes, beginning the intensive indoctrination into obeah that was her primary purpose for the trip. She told Moe, "I have seen things!"[22] She watched old women conduct the sensual learning ritual that would prepare a young virgin for her wedding night. She also participated in two different "Nine Night" ceremonies intended to keep the spirit of the dead—the "duppy"—from returning to haunt the living. One of these ended in a naked, orgiastic dance climaxed by the sacrifice of a goat.

As exciting as these adventures were, after Hurston left Jamaica for Haiti, she discovered an entire system of belief that made Nine Night rituals look like child's play. She arrived in Port-au-Prince in late September. Her Haitian plan was to take a house up in the hills so that she could write during the periods when she was not finding things. She was fortunate in locating such a place, with a maid, Lucille, who was sympathetic and honest. But she was immediately confronted with such a wealth of material that she found it impossible to write up her research. In little less than three months she perfected her Creole, acquired a working knowledge of voodoo gods, attended a number of ceremonies presided over by a voodoo priest, or "houngan," and photographed an apparent zombie.

In December she took a trip to the beautiful Île de la Gonâve, near the harbor of Port-au-Prince. The local belief was that the island was formed when a whale bore a sleeping goddess on his back and that now the goddess held the formula of peace in her hand. Zora found the place enchanted, discovering "a peace I have never known anywhere else on earth." At night the luminous sea glittered like bushels of gems; the days were filled with languor, the air resting heavily on the rich green foliage.[23]

Haiti released a flood of language and emotion that Zora finally admitted to herself had been "dammed up" inside ever since her departure from New York. For seven straight weeks after her arrival she struggled to get it down on paper, sometimes writing late at night after a day of collecting. By the third week in December she had completed her second novel. She sent it to Lippincott's, and when she returned to the United States mainland in March, 1937, plans were already underway for the novel's publication in the fall; the editors had found little need for revisions. The book was to be called *Their Eyes Were Watching God*.[24]

Their Eyes Were Watching God is a love story. The impetus for the tale came from Zora's affair with a man of West Indian parentage whom she had first met in New York in 1931 and then found again during her short-lived attempt at graduate school. The relationship was stormy, perhaps doomed from the first. He could not abide her career, but she could not break away. Her collecting trip with Lomax and her Guggenheim Fellowship were both intended to sever the relationship, to "smother" her feelings; both times her return brought them back together. As she admitted, "The plot was far from the circumstances, but I tried to embalm all the tenderness of my passion for him in *Their Eyes Were Watching God*."

This affair is instructive because it illustrates how Hurston used personal experience for her fiction. *Their Eyes Were Watching God* is autobiographical only in the sense that she managed to capture the emotional essence of a love affair between an older woman and a younger man. The prototype for the man, Tea Cake, was not a laborer, but a college student of twenty-three who had been a member of the cast for *The Great Day*. Handsome, lithe, muscular, he owned a smile that brightened rooms. But he was not a gambler and vagabond like Tea Cake; in fact, he was studying to be a minister, and the two of them held long conversations about religious issues. His quick intelligence and considerable learning no doubt attracted her as much as anything else. What Zora took from this relationship was the quality of its emotion: its tenderness, its intensity, and perhaps its sense of ultimate impossibility. Sooner or later it had to end, and when she left for the West Indies, she did so with a stoic toughness. The man she was leaving remembers that outwardly she was calm and that he was left hurt and confused, wondering if she was "crying on the inside." She gave him her answer in *Their Eyes Were Watching God*.[25]

Whatever its personal matrix, Hurston's novel is much more than an outpouring of private feeling. It is both her most accomplished work of art and the authentic, fictional representation of Eatonville she had been struggling for in *Jonah's Gourd Vine*. The novel culminates the fifteen-year effort to celebrate her birthright, a celebration which came through the exploration of a woman's consciousness, accompanied by an assertion of that woman's right to selfhood. By the time she wrote *Their Eyes Were Watching God*—or perhaps in the act of writing it, struggling to reconcile public career and private emotion—Zora Neale Hurston discovered one of the flaws in her early memories of the village: there had usually been only men telling lies on the front porch of Joe Clarke's store.

Their Eyes Were Watching God is about Janie Crawford, raised by her grandmother to "take a stand on high ground" and be spared the traditional fate reserved for black women as beasts of burden: "Ah been prayin' fuh it tuh be different wid you," Nanny tells her granddaughter. The search to fulfill through Janie her "dream of what a woman oughta be and to do" leads to Logan Killicks, owner of sixty acres, a house, and a mule. Older, looking "like a skullhead in the graveyeard," Killicks marries Janie shortly before the grandmother's death. When the marriage proves loveless, Janie searches for something or someone to represent "sun-up and pollen and blooming trees." She finds Joe Starks, an assertive, self-confident striver on his way to Eatonville, Florida, the town made "all outa colored folks," where a man can be his own boss. Joe intends to become a "big voice," and shortly after their arrival he buys 200 acres of land, sets up a store, secures a post office, and campaigns for mayor. Jody is the kind of man who has "uh throne in de seat of his pants," who "changes everything, but nothin' don't change him." He expects his wife to act like a mayor's wife, keep her place, subordinate herself to her master. The spirit of Janie's second marriage leaves the bedroom and takes "to living in the parlor," and she finally reacts to Joe's constant disparagement by publicly questioning his manhood. He dies a short time later, bitter over her revolt, shaken by the challenge to his authority.

Now a woman of means, Janie is beset by status-conscious suitors; but she rejects her class role and falls in love with Vergible "Tea Cake" Woods, a free-spirited laborer much younger than she. Tea Cake is a "glance from God"; he teaches her "de maiden language all over." To Tea Cake, Janie is the "keys to de kingdom."

Without the hypocrisy and the role-playing that characterized her other marriages, this love is strong enough to make both parties open and giving. Tea Cake accepts Janie as an equal. She travels with him from job to job, even though her money would enable them to settle comfortably in Eatonville. They eventually end up working happily together in the bean fields of the "muck," the rich black land reclaimed from Lake Okeechobee in the Everglades. Their bliss is short lived, for during their escape from a hurricane Tea Cake saves Janie but is bitten by a rabid dog. He develops rabies, and his illness drives him mad; eventually he attempts to shoot Janie. Reacting in self-defense, she shoots back, killing him, and then is tried and acquitted by a white jury. Janie is left at the end with the memories of a transcendent love and a wise awareness of its relativity. Yet she knows that Tea Cake will "never be dead until she herself had finished feeling and thinking."

This ending seems poorly plotted, and the narration shifts awkwardly from first to third person. But on the whole the novel is remarkable, with a consistent richness of imagery. Most critical commentary has either ignored this element or treated it superficially; yet the novel's effect depends largely upon the organic metaphors used to represent Janie's emotional life.[26] The imagery is introduced early, when the sixteen-year-old Janie is at the moment of sexual awakening. Using a symbol which will reappear often, Hurston identifies Janie with a blossoming pear tree. To the girl stretched on her back beneath the tree, the tree seems to represent the mystery of the springtime universe: "From barren brown stems to glistening leaf buds; from the leaf buds to snowy virginity of bloom it stirred her tremendously. How? Why?" As she lies there, soaking in the alto chant of the visiting bees, the mystery is revealed: "The inaudible voice of it all came to her. She saw a dust bearing bee sink into the sanctum of a bloom; the thousand sister calyxes arch to meet the love embrace and the ecstatic shiver of the tree from root to tiniest branch creaming in every blossom and frothing with delight. So this was a marriage! She had been summoned to behold a revelation. Then Janie felt a pain remorseless sweet that left her limp and languid."

The orgasm described here comes to represent the organic union Janie searches for throughout her life: she wants "to be a pear tree—any tree in bloom." Yet events conspire to deny her a feeling of wholeness. Her hand-picked husband, Logan Killicks, is a "vision ... desecrating the pear tree." Joe Starks does not "represent sun-up and pollen and blooming trees," but he does speak for a new life away from Killicks; Janie mistakenly thinks that perhaps he can become "a bee for her bloom." After Joe refuses to recognize Janie's autonomy, she discovers that she has "no more blossomy openings dusting pollen over her man, neither any glistening young fruit where the petals used to be." Tea Cake, however, embodies the organic union of completion: "He could be a bee to a blossom—a pear tree blossom in the spring. He seemed to be crushing scent out of the world with his footsteps." Tea Cake's only material legacy is a package of seeds he had meant to plant before his death. Janie vows to plant them for remembrance, commemorating the organic unity of their marriage with a living monument.

This organic imagery permeates the novel and suggests a resolution of time and space, man and nature, subject and object, life and death. In an episode borrowed from "Mule Bone," Hurston tells of a local mule, legendary for its meanness, that dies and is given a burial by the village. Dragging the mule to the swamp, the town makes a "great ceremony" of the interment with speeches and singing; one man even imitates John Pearson preaching a funeral sermon. They mock "everything human in death," then leave the mule to the buzzards. In a surrealistic scene, startling in a realistic novel, Hurston reports on the buzzards' conversation as the birds pick out the eyes "in the ceremonial way" and then go about their feast. Some commentators have criticized this scene for being an imposition of folklore on the narrative; but it is as natural for buzzards to speak as for bees to pollinate flowers, as for a human being to be a "natural man."[27] When not a part of the organic process of birth, growth, and death, one is out of rhythm with the universe. This is represented in the novel by Janie's dissociation of sensibility before she grows to consciousness. She discovers that "she had an inside and an outside now and suddenly she knew how not to mix them." She can sit and watch "the shadow of herself going about tending store and prostrating herself before Jody," but all the time "she herself is sitting under a shady tree with the wind blowing through her hair." Jody denies Janie participation in the mule's burial, and the restriction illustrates how she is out of touch with the cadence of nature. She tells Joe that "in some way we ain't natural wid one 'nother'." Later, with Tea Cake, Janie feels in time natural process, just as she did under the pear tree as a child.

One might argue that Janie's finding the one true bee for her blossom is hardly a satisfactory response from a liberated woman. But the action is symbolic, demonstrating Janie's ability to grow into an adult awareness of self, and it is not until the imagery of the pear tree fuses with the motif of the horizon that this symbolic action is completed. Janie's romantic "dreams" of the pear tree are tempered by growth and time. What was thought to be the truth at puberty is gradually transformed by experience. Her childhood had ended when a neighbor boy failed to fulfill her romantic dreams. Killicks initiated her further, showing that "marriage did not make love. Janie's first dream was dead. So she became a woman." Joe Starks took Killicks's place, but Joe was a false dream too, "just something she had grabbed up to drape her dreams over." It is not until Tea Cake that her dream—now toughened by knowledge—can become truth. The reason is that Tea Cake suggests the horizon—he is the "son of Evening Sun"—and the horizon motif illustrates the distance one must travel in order to distinguish between illusion and reality, dream and truth, role and self.

Hurston claims at the beginning of the novel that men and women dream differently. For men, "ships at a distance have every man's wish on board. For some they come in with the tide. For others they sail forever on the horizon, never out of sight, never landing until the Watcher turns his eyes in resignation, his dreams mocked to death by time." Women, however, believe that the horizon is close at hand, willing it so: "Now women forget all those things they don't want to remember and remember everything they don't want to forget. The dream is the truth. Then they act and do things accordingly."

This complicated opening passage begins to make sense midway into the book, when Janie comes to an awareness that her grandmother has pointed her in the wrong direction:

> She had been getting ready for her great journey to the horizons in search of *people*; it was important to all the world that she should find them and they find her. But she had been whipped like a cur dog, and run off down a back road after *things*. It was all according to the way you see things. Some people could look at a mud-puddle and see an ocean with ships. But Nanny belonged to that other kind that loved to deal in scraps. Here Nanny had taken the biggest thing God ever made, the horizon—for no matter how far a person can go the horizon is still way beyond you—and pinched it in to such a little bit of a thing that she could tie it about her granddaughter's neck tight enough to choke her.

This second passage parallels the first in imagery and diction, demonstrating Janie's growing self-confidence in her own judgments and her realistic appraisal of her failed dreams. Only when thus prepared can she accept Tea Cake as an equal, without illusion, discovering love because she is finally accepted for herself. Tea Cake is certainly not an ideal husband, but he does grant Janie the dignity of self. On the final pages of *Their Eyes Were Watching God* Janie tells her friend, Pheoby, "Ah done been tuh de horizon and back and now ah kin set heah in mah house and live by comparisons." She has experienced the reality rather than dreamed it—"you got tuh *go* there tuh *know* there," she says—which means that the novel can end with an imagistic resolution of the distance between here and there, self and horizon. Escaping from a horizon that can be tied tight enough to choke, Janie peacefully gathers in the world: "She pulled in her horizon like a great fish-net. Pulled it from around the waist of the world and draped it over her shoulder. So much of life in its meshes! She called in her soul to come and see."

Janie's poetic self-realization is inseparable from Zora's concomitant awareness of her cultural situation. The novel also celebrates the black woman's liberation from a legacy of degradation. Janie's grandmother had given wrong directions because of her historical experience; she wants her granddaughter to marry Logan Killicks because of her own slave memories: "Ah didn't want to be used for a work-ox and a brood sow.... It sho wasn't mah will for things to happen lak they did." Janie's mother was also born into slavery, the offspring of the master, and Nanny had hoped that Emancipation would bring her daughter freedom. But she is raped by her schoolteacher, and Janie is conceived in the violence. Her mother leaves home a ruined woman, destroyed in spirit. Janie is left with Nanny, who sees the child as another chance: "Ah wanted to preach a great sermon about colored women sittin' on high, but they wasn't no pulpit for me.... Ah been waitin a long time, Janie, but nothin' Ah been through ain't too much if you just take a stance on high ground lak ah dreamed." Nanny "can't die easy thinkin' maybe de men folks white or black is makin a spit cup outa yuh." To her, Logan Killicks is "big protection" from this vision; when Janie complains about the absence of love, her grandmother responds, "Dis love! Dat's just whut's got us [black women] uh pullin' and uh haulin' and sweatin' and doin from can't see in de mornin' til can't see at night."

Janie has, therefore, both a historical and a personal memory to react against in her search for autonomy. Much of the novel is concerned with her struggle to understand the inadequacy of her grandmother's vision. Tea Cake is not the means to self-understanding, only the partner of Janie's liberation from an empty way of living; she tells Pheoby: "Ah done lived Grandma's way, now ah means to live mine." Asked to explain, Janie says,

> She was borned in slavery time when folks, dat is black folks, didn't sit down anytime dey felt lak it. So sittin' on porches lak de white madam looked lak uh mighty fine thing tuh her. Dat's whut she wanted for me—don't keer whut it cost. Git upon uh high chair and sit dere. She didn't have time tuh think whut tuh do after you got up on de stool uh do nothin. De object wuz tuh git dere. So Ah got up on de high stool lak she told me, but Pheoby, Ah done nearly languished tuh death up dere. Ah felt like de world wuz cryin' extry and Ah ain't read de common news yet.

The vertical metaphor in this speech represents Hurston's entire system of thought, her social and racial philosophy. People erred because they wanted to be *above* others, an impulse which eventually led to denying the humanity of those below. Whites had institutionalized such thinking, and black people were vulnerable to the philosophy because being on high like white folks seemed to represent security and power. Janie's grandmother had believed that "de white man is de ruler of everything as fur as ah been able tuh find out." She thinks that freedom is symbolized by achieving the position on high. Zora Hurston had always known, just as Janie discovers, that there was no air to breathe up there. She had always identified with what she called "the poor Negro, the real one in the furrows and cane breaks." She bitterly criticized black leaders who ignored this figure while seeking "a few paltry dollars and some white person's tea table." She once wrote that in her opinion some black leaders wanted most to be able to return from a meeting and say, "No other Negro was present besides me." This sense of racial pride had contributed much to *Their Eyes Were Watching God*; "I am on fire about my people. I need not concern myself with the few individuals who have quit the race via the tea table."[28]

Zora Neale Hurston had spent an entire career chronicling the cultural life of "the Negro farthest down," the beauty and wisdom of "the people"; she did not find racial liberation in the terms of white domination, or selfhood for the black woman in the arrogance of male supremacy. Black people became free not by emulating whites, but by building from the cultural institutions of the black community; women discovered an organic relationship with men only when there was consent between equals. This is the key to Janie's relationship with Tea Cake. In their very first meeting Janie apologizes for not being able to play checkers; no one has taught her how. She is surprised to discover that Tea Cake wants her to play, that he "thought it natural for her to play." When she resorts to role-playing in the competition, coyly asking him not to jump her exposed king, he jumps anyway, applying the rules of the game equally. In similar fashion they share the labor of the fields and the hardships of migrant life. While Jody would not let her take part in storytelling sessions, with Tea Cake it is perfectly natural for her to be a participant in oral tradition: "The men held big arguments here like they used to do on the store porch. Only here she could listen and laugh and even talk some herself if she wanted to. She got so she could tell big stories herself from listening to the rest." It is important to note that Janie's participation comes after she has learned to recognize sexism, a necessary preliminary to her self-discovery. In the lying sessions on Joe's store porch, the philosophy of male dominance, often a part of black folklore, was everywhere present. Somebody had to think for "women and chillun and chickens and cows." Men saw one thing and understood ten, while women saw ten things and understood none. Janie eventually informs this male enclave that they will be surprised if they "ever find out yuh don't know half as much about us as you think you do." Her later life with Tea Cake, freely contracted for, without illusion (Tea Cake can be sexist, too), is a natural result of this developing consciousness.

Janie's verbal freedom might not seem such an important matter on the surface, but the reader should remember Hurston's conception of the store porch as a stage for the presentation of black folklore. The one time in the novel Janie takes over this male sanctuary, she is praised by the storytellers for being a "born orator. Us never knowed dat befo'. She put jus' de right words tuh our thoughts." However, Joe's sense of wifely propriety does not permit her repeat performances, and although "Janie loved the conversation and sometimes she thought up good stories," her husband forbids her to indulge. The storytellers are "trashy," because they lack his drive. As Janie later realized, "Jody classed me off."

When Hurston writes of Eatonville, the store porch is all-important. It is the center of the community, the totem representing black cultural tradition; it is where the values of the group are manifested in verbal behavior. The store porch, in Zora's language is "the center of the world." To describe the porch's activities she often uses the phrase "crayon enlargements of life"—"When the people sat around on the porch and passed around the pictures of their thoughts for the others to look at and see, it was nice. The fact that the thought pictures were always crayon enlargements of life made it even nicer to listen to." It is on the store porch that the lying competition takes place, "a contest in hyperbole and carried out for no other reason." Borrowing from the verbal competition over Daisy in "Mule Bone," Hurston uses the store porch as the center of a courtship ritual which provides the town with amusement. Yet they know it's not courtship. It's acting out courtship and everybody is in the play. The store porch is where "big picture talkers" use "a side of the world for a canvas" as they create a portrait of communal values.

The rhythms and natural imagery which structure the novel refer not only to liberation from sexual roles but also to the self-fulfillment inherent in this sense of community. Janie's "blossoming refers personally to her discovery of self and ultimately to her meaningful participation in black tradition. Janie discovers a way to make use of the traditions of slavery—her grandmother's memories—not by seeking to "class off" and attempt to "sit on high" as the white folks did, but by celebrating blackness. She asks the color-struck Mrs. Turner, "We'se uh mingled people and all of us got black kinfolks as well as yaller kinfolks. How come you so against black?" June Jordan calls *Their Eyes Were Watching God* the "most successful, convincing and exemplary novel of blacklove that we have. Period."[29] She is speaking of Janie's growth into awareness of the possibilities of love—between black men and black women—both individually and collectively, as selves and as members of a racial community.

Their Eyes Were Watching God responds in subtle ways to the criticism Zora had received. Certainly not a protest novel in the tradition of Richard Wright, parts of the book do capture the "smouldering resentment" of the black South. After the hurricane's destruction, a natural disaster the races suffer together, the white authorities are quick to reimpose supremacy by conscripting black men to bury the victims in segregated graves. Janie's trial has an arrogance about it; her freedom depends on the sanction of twelve white men who simply cannot understand her relationship with Tea Cake. The trial, however, is not grafted to the book to demonstrate the inequity of southern justice. It serves, rather, to illustrate the depth of Janie's discovery of self; for not only is she faced with a white power-structure irrelevant to her feelings, she is also blamed for the killing by Tea Cake's friends. She is not supposed to have the right of self-defense; they murmur that "uh white man and uh nigger woman is de freest thing on earth. Dey do as dey please." This is literally true for Janie, but only because she has become a complete woman, no longer divided between an inner and an outer self—a woman at home with the natural cycles of birth and death, love and loss, knowledge and selfhood. Janie's growth is Hurston's subject. Although that growth is affected by the racism surrounding her, white oppression is not the dominant factor in Janie's development. Zora is saying once again that it is arrogant for whites to think that black lives are only defensive reactions to white actions.

This very complicated argument was misinterpreted by almost all the novel's reviewers. The white establishment failed to recognize that her subject was purposefully chosen; they liked the story, but usually for the wrong reasons. Hershel Brickell in the *New York Post* compared Hurston favorably to D. H. Lawrence in her depiction of sensory experience. The *Saturday Review* called the novel "a simple and unpretentious story, but there is nothing else quite like it." Richard Wright, a Communist party member at the time, reviewed it for *New Masses*, complaining bitterly about the minstrel image that he claimed she was perpetuating. He admitted that "her dialogue manages to catch the psychological movements of the Negro folk-mind in their pure simplicity"; but as a Marxist intellectual working for social change, he felt that was counterrevolutionary. As with Sterling Brown, the lack of bitterness offended Wright: "Her characters eat and laugh and cry and work and kill; they swing like a pendulum eternally in that safe and narrow orbit in which America likes to see the Negro live: between laughter and tears."[30]

Wright's review had to hurt, and it no doubt fed Zora's lifelong suspicion of communism. But the review that infuriated came well after publication, in Alain Locke's January, 1938, *Opportunity* survey of the previous year's "literature by and about the Negro." Locke called the title magical and praised Zora's "cradle-gift" for storytelling. But he criticized the book because folklore was its "main point." Admittedly, it was "folklore fiction at its best"; but when was Hurston going to "come to grips with motive fiction and social document fiction"? Modern southern fiction had to get rid of condescension as well as oversimplification.

Zora's response was to write a malicious, angry portrait of Locke, which she insisted *Opportunity* publish, and which they wisely refused. Openly libelous, the attack was unfair; the intensity of the invective was characteristic of the Hurston temper. She called the review "an example of rank dishonesty" and "a conscious fraud." She claimed that Locke "knows that he knows nothing about Negroes" and that he "pants to be a leader"; yet "up to now, Dr. Locke has not produced one single idea or suggestion of an idea that he can call his own." Her specific objection was to Locke's complaint that folklore intruded in the novel, detracting from the fiction, and she was enraged by his implication that the author condescended to her folk subjects. Zora claimed, in typical overstatement, that "there is not a folk tale in the entire book." She proposed, "I will send my toe-nails to debate him on what he knows about Negroes and Negro life, and I will come personally to debate him on what he knows about literature on the subject. This one who lives by quotations trying to criticize people who live by life." She felt that it was Locke, the Harvard Ph.D. and Oxford scholar, who condescended when he referred to the "pseudo-primitives" who were her folk characters.[31]

All of this was directed at a man who had helped Zora often. It shows the frustration of an author whose novelistic talents were deprecated because her fiction dealt with intraracial folkloric situations rather than with interracial confrontations—it was not "social document fiction." The difference in these perspectives is not between protest and accommodation, as Wright implied, but between different conceptions of the folk community. The difference is illustrated on the first page of *Their Eyes Were Watching God*. Janie has returned to Eatonville to tell her story; it is sundown and people are sitting on their porches: "It was the time to hear things and talk. These sitters had been tongueless, earless, eyeless, conveniences all day long. Mules and other brutes had occupied their skins. But now the sun and the bossman were gone, so the skins felt powerful and human." Just as Janie's struggle is to move beyond Nanny's observation that a black woman is "the mule of the world" into an awareness of her own humanity, so is Hurston's subject men rather than mules. Zora wrote of black life after the warrior stances preserving self-dignity in a hostile environment have been set aside for community fellowship. Folklore transmission is a natural product of this sense of security, for it is on these front porches that one's image can be turned from a negative to a positive identification ("I'm like that old mule / Black and don't give a damn / You got to take me / Like I Am"). Locke denied the validity of Zora's fictional environment when he claimed that she imposed folklore on reality rather than represented reality itself. It was natural for her response to be excessive, for she perceived a threat to her entire fictional world. Her fiction represented the processes of folkloric transmission, emphasizing the ways of thinking and speaking which grew from the folk environment. But it was fiction, not folklore. Zora replied to Locke by asserting, "To his discomfort I must say that those lines came out of my own head." Like Janie reacting to Joe Starks, Zora Hurston was claiming her right to an autonomous imagination, both as a woman and as a member of the black American community. She was reacting in defense of a people who had been stereotyped as pseudoprimitive minstrels.[32]

NOTES

1. ZNH, transcript of employment (National Personnel Records Center, WPA Federal Theatre Project, New York City).

2. Jonathan Daniels, "Black Magic and Dark Laughter," *Saturday Review*, Oct. 19, 1935, p. 12; H. I. Brock, "The Full, True Flavor of Life in a Negro Community," *New York Times*, Nov. 10, 1935, p. 4; Henry Lee Moon, "Big Old Lies," *New Republic*, Dec. 11, 1935, p. 142.

3. Unidentified clipping, Sterling Brown, review of *Mules and Men*, Feb. 25, 1936 (JWJYale).

4. Ibid.

5. For Hurston's comments on the publisher's demands for *Mules and Men* see ZNH to CVV, Mar. 24, 1934 (JWJYale), and ZNH, "What White Publishers Won't Print," *Negro Digest*, 8 (Apr., 1950), 85–89. For the Ocoee riot story see "The Ocoee Riot," typescript; possibly by ZNH, Florida Federal Writers' Project (FHSP).

6. "Zora Neale Hurston," in *Twentieth Century Authors*, ed. Stanley Kunitz and Howard Haycraft (New York: H. W. Wilson, 1942), pp. 694–95.

7. Harold Preece, "The Negro Folk Cult," *Crisis*, 43 (1936), 364, 374.

8. Ibid.

9. See Alan Dundes's notes to Preece, "Negro Folk Cult," reprinted in *Mother Wit from the Laughing Barrel* (Englewood Cliffs, N.J.: Prentice-Hall, 1973) p. 37; LH, "Me and the Mule," *Negro Quarterly*, 1 (1942), 37.

10. ZNH, "Characteristics of Negro Expression," in *Negro: An Anthology*, ed. Nancy Cunard (London: Wishart, 1934), p. 39.

11. June Jordan, "On Richard Wright and Zora Neale Hurston," *Black World* 23 (Aug., 1974), 5.

12. ZNH, "The Fiery Chariot," typescript play in one act (HCUFla). This is described in the program for *From Sun to Sun*, Feb. 11, 1933, as "an original Negro folk-play (a folk-tale dramatized by Zora Hurston)."

13. Gladys-Marie Fry, *Night Riders* (Knoxville: University of Tennessee Press, 1975).

14. ZNH, "Characteristics of Negro Expression," pp. 41, 42, 43, 46.

15. "Says Race is Gifted," *St. Louis Argus*, Oct. 19, 1934 (report of a ZNH speech) (Schomburg Collection, New York Public Library).

16. "WPA Productions Scheduled by Rice," *New York Times*, Dec. 17, 1935, p. 30; ZNH to Edwin Osgood Grover, Dec. 29, 1935 (HCUFla); ZNH, application for John Simon Guggenheim Fellowship, Nov. 15, 1935 (GgFnd); employment transcript, "Zora Neale Hurston, WPA Federal Theatre Project, New York City" (National Personnel Records Center); ZNH to Henry Allen Moe of the Guggenheim Foundation, Mar. 18, 1936 (GgFnd).

17. ZNH to Henry Allen Moe, n.d. [received Apr. 20, 1936]; "U.S. Woman Anthropologist on Hoodoo Hunt in Jamaica," *Kingston Daily Gleaner*, Apr. 24, 1936; ZNH to Moe, n.d. [received May 5, 1936] (GgFnd). Quotations in this reconstruction of Hurston's expedition to Haiti that are not noted come from her *Tell My Horse* (Philadelphia: J. B. Lippincott, 1938).

18. ZNH to Henry Allen Moe, May 22, 28, June 10, 1936 (GgFnd).

19. Ibid., May 22, 1936 (GgFnd).

20. ZNH, *Tell My Horse*, p. 36. Compare Hurston's account of the Maroons with Katharine Dunham's in *Journey to Accompong* (New York: Henry Holt, 1946).

21. ZNH to Henry Allen Moe, May 22, June 10, 1936 (GgFnd).

22. Ibid., Sept. 24, 1936 (GgFnd).

23. ZNH, *Tell My Horse*, p. 158.

24. ZNH to Henry Allen Moe, Mar. 20, July 6, 1937 (GgFnd); RH interview with Bertram Lippincott, Dec. 17, 1970, Penllyn, Pa.; RH interviews with Tay Hohoff, Dec., 1970, May, 1971, New York City. The manuscript of *Their Eyes Were Watching God* is dated Dec. 19, 1936 (JWJYale).

25. RH interview with "P" (name withheld by request), Jan. 15, 1976, New York City.

26. *Their Eyes Were Watching God* has received much critical treatment. Readers may wish to compare my own interpretation with the following: Jordan, "On Richard Wright and Zora Neale Hurston," pp. 4–10; Ellease Southerland, "Zora Neale Hurston," *Black World*, 23 (Aug., 1974), 20–30; Emma L. Blake, "Zora Neale Hurston: Author and Folklorist," *Negro History Bulletin*, 29 (Apr., 1966), 149–50, 165; Robert Bone, *The Negro Novel in America* (New Haven: Yale University Press,

1958), pp. 126–32; James W. Byrd, "Zora Neale Hurston: A Novel Folklorist," *Tennessee Folklore Society Bulletin*, 21 (1955), 37–41; Ralph Ellison, "Recent Negro Fiction," *New Masses*, Aug. 5, 1941, pp. 22–26; Hugh Gloster, *Negro Voices in American Fiction* (Chapel Hill: University of North Carolina Press, 1948), pp. 235–37; Evelyn Thomas Helmick, "Zora Neale Hurston," *Carrell*, 11 (June and Dec., 1970), 1–19; Ann Rayson, "The Novels of Zora Neale Hurston," *Studies in Black Literature*, 5 (Winter, 1974), 1–11; S. Jay Walker, "Zora Neale Hurston's *Their Eyes Were Watching God*: Black Novel of Sexism," *Modern Fiction Studies*, 20 (Winter, 1974–75), 519–27; Darwin T. Turner, *In a Minor Chord* (Carbondale: Southern Illinois University Press, 1971); Adam David Miller, "Some Observations on a Black Aesthetic," in *New Black Voices*, ed. Abraham Chapman (New York: Signet, 1972), p. 541; Roger Rosenblatt, *Black Fiction* (Cambridge: Harvard University Press, 1974); James O. Young, *Black Writers of the Thirties* (Baton Rouge: Louisiana State University Press, 1973), pp. 219–23; James R. Giles, "The Significance of Time in Zora Neale Hurston's *Their Eyes Were Watching God*," *Negro American Literature Forum*, 6 (Summer, 1972), 52–53, 60; Mary Helen Washington, "The Black Woman's Search for Identity," *Black World*, 21 (Aug., 1972) 68–75; Addison Gayle, *The Way of the New World* (Garden City, N.Y.: Doubleday, 1976), pp. 168–80. The last two critics cited are among the best commentators on the novel.

27. Turner, *In a Minor Chord*, p. 106.

28. ZNH to Mrs. Mason, Oct. 15, 1931 (HUAL).

29. Jordan, "On Richard Wright and Zora Neale Hurston," p. 6.

30. Herschel Brickell, review of *Their Eyes Were Watching God*, *New York Post*, Sept. 14, 1937; George Stevens, "Negroes by Themselves," *Saturday Review*, Sept. 18, 1937, p. 3; Richard Wright, "Between Laughter and Tears," *New Masses*, Oct. 5, 1937. Wright's conception of folkloric fiction was more complicated than his review suggests; see his "Blueprint for Negro Writing," *New Challenge*, 2 (Fall, 1937), 53–65.

31. ZNH, "The Chick with One Hen," typescript (JWJYale). See also ZNH to James Weldon Johnson, n.d. [ca. Feb., 1938] (JWJYale).

32. LH, "Me and the Mule," *Negro Quarterly*, 1 (1942), 37; ZNH, "Chick with One Hen."

CHERYL A. WALL

Zora Neale Hurston:
Changing Her Own Words

The developing tradition of black women's writing nurtured now in the
prose and poetry of such writers as Toni Morrison and Alice Walker
began with the work of Zora Neale Hurston. Hurston was not the first
Afro-American woman to publish a novel, but she was the first to create
language and imagery that reflected the reality of black women's lives.
Ignoring the stereotypes, social and literary, that her predecessors spent
their energies rejecting, Hurston rooted her art in the cultural traditions
of the black rural South. As a daughter of the region, she claimed these
traditions by birthright. As an anthropologist, she reclaimed them
through years of intense, often perilous, research. As a novelist, she
summoned this legacy in her choice of setting, her delineation of
character, and most devotedly in her distillation of language. Hers
became the first authentic black female voice in American literature.

Despite this achievement, Hurston's work suffered years of
obscurity and critical neglect. Ten years ago, outside of that small group
of readers and scholars whose primary devotion is to Afro-American
literature, few had even heard her name. Still fewer were able to read her
work, as it had been out of print since long before her death in 1960.
Today Hurston's work has been revived, her reputation restored. She is
now considered one of the major writers to have emerged from the
Harlem Renaissance. Moreover, hers is the pre-eminent achievement in

From *Zora Neale Hurston: Critical Perspectives Past and Present*, edited by Henry Louis
Gates, Jr. and K.A. Appiah. © 1993 by Cheryl A. Wall. Reprinted by permission.

Afro-American letters during the 1930s; five of her seven books were published in that decade. Two of these, the folklore collection, *Mules and Men* (1935), and the novel, *Their Eyes Were Watching God* (1937), are now recognized classics in the Afro-American canon. The novel is becoming a favorite in American literature and women's studies courses as well. Although very much of its time, *Their Eyes Were Watching God* is timeless. As Sherley Anne Williams has written, its heroine's "individual quest for fulfillment becomes any woman's tale."[1] Other scholars and critics have begun to analyze Hurston's fiction in numerous articles and essays. The fascinating but hitherto fragmented story of her life has been reconstructed in a meticulously researched biography. Although her work is not nearly as well known as it deserves to be, more people have read it in the last few years than in Hurston's lifetime. For general readers and scholars alike, Zora Neale Hurston has emerged as a writer who must be taken seriously.

The black consciousness and feminist movements spurred the rediscovery and reassessment of Hurston's work. Under this impetus, her work began to be reprinted in the 1960s; it garnered little attention initially, overlooked in the flood of books by black writers suddenly returned to print. More of her books became available in the 1970s, often republished with introductions by leading black scholars and critics. By this time, feminists were retrieving works by "lost" women writers, a category for which Hurston was eminently qualified. Hurston's strong, resilient female characters won further favor; the first anthology of her prose, edited by Alice Walker, carried the imprint of the Feminist Press. Walker, whose championing of Hurston has been unselfish and unstinting, surely spoke for others when she wrote, "I became aware of my need of Zora Neale Hurston some time before I knew her work existed."[2] Walker explained that she found in Hurston a conviction of "racial health"; Hurston's characters were invaluable because of their ability to accept and love themselves.

The critical perspectives inspired by the black consciousness and feminist movements allow us to see Hurston's writings in a new way. They correct distorted views of her folklore as charming and quaint, set aside misperceptions of her characters as minstrels caught, in Richard Wright's phrase, "between laughter and tears."[3] These new perspectives inform this re-evaluation of Hurston's work. She asserted that black people, while living in a racist society that denied their humanity, had created an alternative culture that validated their worth as human beings. Although that culture was in some respects sexist, black women, like black men, attained personal identity not by transcending the culture but by embracing it.

Hurston's respect for the cultural traditions of black people is the most important constant in her career. This respect threads through her entire oeuvre, linking the local-color short fiction of her youth, her ethnographic research in the rural South and the Caribbean (an account of her fieldwork in Jamaica and Haiti, *Tell My Horse*, was published in 1938), her novels, and the essays she contributed to popular journals in her later years. In all, she published more than fifty short stories and articles in addition to her book-length works. Because her focus was on black cultural traditions, she rarely explored interracial themes. The black/white conflict, which loomed paramount in the fiction of her black contemporaries, in Wright's novels especially, hardly surfaced in Hurston's. Poet and critic June Jordan has described how the absence of explicitly political protest caused Hurston's work to be devalued. Affirmation, not protest, is Hurston's hallmark. Yet, as Jordan argues, "affirmation of black values and lifestyle within the American context is, indeed, an act of protest."[4] Hurston appreciated and approved the reluctance of blacks to reveal "that which the soul lives by" to the hostile and uncomprehending gaze of outsiders. But the interior reality was what she wished to probe. In that reality, blacks ceased to be "tongueless, earless, eyeless conveniences" whose labor whites exploited; they ceased to be mules and were men and women.

The survival of the spirit was proclaimed first and foremost through language. As a writer, Hurston was keenly sensitive to the richness of black verbal expression. Like Langston Hughes and Sterling Brown, she had no patience with theories of linguistic deficiency among blacks; she ignored racist assumptions that rural blacks spoke as they did because they were too stupid to learn standard English. Hurston, whose father was a Baptist preacher, was well acquainted with the tradition of verbal elegance among black people. From her father's example, she perceived how verbal agility conferred status within the community. His sermons had demonstrated as well the power of his language to convey the complexity of the lives of his parishioners. Early in her career, Hurston attempted to delineate "characteristics of Negro expression." She stressed the heightened sense of drama revealed in the preference for action words and the "will to adorn" reflected in the profusion of metaphor and simile, and in the use of double descriptives (*low-down*) and verbal nouns (*funeralize*). To her, the "will to adorn" bespoke a feeling "that there can never be enough of beauty, let alone too much." Zora Hurston shared that feeling, as the beautifully poetic prose of her novels attests. The collective folk expression was the soil that nourished the individual expression of her novels. After a lengthy dialogue with her homefolk, Hurston was prepared to change some words of her own.[5]

In one of her first published articles, Hurston declared:

> BUT I AM NOT tragically colored. There is no great sorrow dammed up in my soul, nor lurking behind my eyes. I do not mind at all. I do not belong to the sobbing school of Negrohood who hold that nature somehow has given them a lowdown dirty deal and whose feelings are all hurt about it.... No, I do not weep at the world—I am too busy sharpening my oyster knife.[6]

The exuberant tone of the assertions in "How It Feels to Be Colored Me" suggests that they were more strongly felt than reasoned. Hurston locates the source of her feelings in her childhood experiences in Eatonville, Florida, the hometown to which she often returned in fiction and fact. Eatonville was an all-black town, the first to be incorporated in the United States. Hurston remembered it as a place of possibility and promise. She revered the wit and wisdom of the townspeople, admired the originality of their culture and their moral and aesthetic values, saw in their language drama and the "will to adorn." Having been insulated from racism in her early years, unaware of racial distinctions until she was nine, she professed herself "astonished" rather than angered by discrimination. The lingering astonishment accounts perhaps for the shortcomings of the article as self and racial definition; Hurston relied on "exotic primitive" myths, popular in the twenties to round out the explanation of herself and her people.

During this time Hurston was studying anthropology at Barnard under the tutelage of Franz Boas. This study complemented by fieldwork in Florida and Louisiana allowed her to appreciate her past intellectually as well as intuitively. No longer were her homefolk simply good storytellers, whose values were commendable, superstitions remarkable, and humor penetrating. As such, they had been well suited for local-color fiction of the kind Hurston published in the 1920s. Now however, "they became a part of cultural anthropology; scientific objects who could and should be studied for their academic value."[7] The cultural relativity of anthropology freed Hurston from the need to defend her subjects' alleged inferiority. She could discard behavioral explanations drawn from racial mythology. Eatonville blacks were neither exotic nor primitive; they had simply selected different characteristics from what Ruth Benedict, another pioneering anthropologist trained by Boas, called the "great arc of human potentialities."

In possession of these liberating theories, Hurston set forth in 1927 on the first of a series of field expeditions. Not surprisingly her first stop was Eatonville, a site she confidently expected to yield a rich lode of material. When the results of her fieldwork were published in *Mules and Men*, she introduced the book by stating, "I was glad when somebody told me, 'you may go and collect Negro folk-lore.'"[8] Her attitude was not typical of a professional anthropologist and neither was her method. She immersed herself in the culture she studied. Sitting on the porch of Joe Clarke's store in Eatonville, later signing on at sawmill camps and apprenticing herself to hoodoo doctors, she became a member of each community she entered. Clearly her race and personal heritage gave her an entrée previous researchers lacked. Beyond that, Hurston felt herself part and parcel of the culture she investigated. The diligence and skill with which she pursued her studies enabled her to capitalize on these advantages.

Mules and Men holds the distinction of being the first collection of Afro-American folklore published by an Afro-American. It distinguishes itself in other ways. Alan Lomax called it "the most engaging, genuine, and skillfully written book in the field of folklore."[9] Unlike many of its predecessors, it presents the lore not to patronize or demean but to affirm and celebrate. Written for a popular audience, it is highly readable; after nearly half a century, it has lost none of its capacity to delight. *Mules and Men* contains seventy folktales, but it is more than a transcription of individual texts. As her biographer Robert Hemenway points out, Hurston adds an unifying narrative that provides contexts as well as texts. By showing when a story is told, how, and to what purpose, Hurston attempts to restore the original meanings of the tales.

Folktales, she understood, serve a function more significant than more entertainment; "they are profound expressions of a group's behavior."[10] They cannot be comprehended without reference to those whose values and beliefs they embody. Consequently, the tales in *Mules and Men* are not collected from faceless informants, but from real men and women whose lives readers are briefly invited to share. Sharing their lives more profoundly, Hurston was ultimately forced to confront the role of women in rural black life. Her response, necessarily personal and engaged, gave shape to her most successful fiction.

Hurston met the woman who most informed this response soon after she arrived in Polk County, Florida, in January 1928. The sawmill camp where Hurston settled was an even richer repository of the folktales, worksongs, blues and cries, proverbs and sermons than Eatonville had been. And of the people who lived there, Big Sweet was the most memorable. Hurston devoted several pages of her autobiography, *Dust Tracks on a Road* (1942), to her friendship with this woman; the influence of Big Sweet is highly visible in characters in Hurston's novels. Although Hurston gives few details about her appearance, the woman's name, with its suggestions of physical power and sexual attractiveness, of strength and tenderness, aptly sums up her character. Significantly, Hurston hears her before she sees her, and it is her talk that attracts her attention. Big Sweet is "specifying," "playing the dozens" with an outmatched male opponent. Before a large and appreciative audience, she breaks the news to him "in one of her mildest bulletins that his pa was a double-humpted camel and his ma a grass-gut cow." This performance gives Hurston "a measure of this Big Sweet," and her judgment is soon verified by the opinions of others on the job. Though fearsome, Big Sweet is not feared as much as she is respected, because the community draws a distinction between meanness and the defense of one's integrity. Hurston sees the wisdom of acquiring her friendship and hence protection. Big Sweet becomes the author's guardian and guide. She identifies informants, awards prizes in "lying" contests, and eventually saves Hurston's life.[11]

In his article, "Negotiating Respect: Patterns of Presentation among Black Women," folklorist Roger Abrahams notes: "how women assert their image and values as women is seldom found in the folklore literature."[12] In keeping with this premise, Big Sweet contributes only two folktales to *Mules and Men*; neither focuses on female identity. The relative scarcity of woman-centered tales in the oral tradition must have been one of the revelations of Hurston's fieldwork. Although tales created by men about women, many of them virulently antifemale, exist in some quantity, tales about women told from a female point of view are rare.[13] Hurston's narrative strategy permits her to sustain a female perspective in her account of Big Sweet. Her presentation of the context as well as the text of the lore is crucial in this regard. In the general narrative of her experiences in Polk County and in her descriptions of the specific situations in which stories are told, Hurston shows how Big Sweet asserts and maintains her identity. From these descriptions, the reader can take her own measure of this woman.

The dramatic performance of Big Sweet's "specifying" is not recounted in *Mules and Men*; her entrance here is low-keyed. She tells her two tales, "Why the Mocking Bird Is Away on Friday" and "How the 'Gator Got Black," matter-of-factly, but the second is preceded by an exchange that reveals a bit of her mettle. Someone else has recited "How Brer 'Gator Got His Tongue Worn Out" which has reminded Big Sweet of the similar tale she knows. Thus the reader sees one way the lore is transmitted. Before she gets a chance to begin her story, however, Big Sweet is interrupted and must reclaim her place in the discussion. "When Ah'm shellin' my corn, you keep out yo' nubbins" wins her readmission and the tale is told. A bit later, as the others joke and lie good-naturedly, Big Sweet injects a personal and pointed warning to her lover not to repeat his infidelity of the night before. He appeals to the other men for assistance, but they cannot beat her "specifying." Her declaration of independence cuts right to the heart of the matter: "Lemme tell *you* something, *any* time Ah shack up wid any man Ah gives myself de privilege to go wherever he might be, night or day. Ah got de law in my mouth."[14]

Big Sweet's behavior conforms to a pattern Abrahams outlines. Respect in the black community is not a permanent given; it must constantly be earned and negotiated. For women, these negotiations usually occur, as in the scenes described above, when people are "just talking." No one, whatever her reputation, is beyond challenge. "Ideally a woman has the ability to *talk sweet* with her infants and peers but *talk smart* or *cold* with anyone who might threaten her self-image."[15] Big Sweet exemplifies this ideal. She uses "Little-Bit" as a term of endearment for the narrator Zora in *Mules and Men*, warns her that collecting songs from one of the men has provoked his lover's jealousy, and promises to defend her. A conversation between her and Hurston quoted in *Dust Tracks* further evidences her ability to "talk sweet." Not understanding why Hurston wants to collect "lies" (folktales), she pledges to aid her in doing so. Such conversations are held privately; the public smart talking she does earns Big Sweet respect. A crucial incident recounted in *Mules and Men* pits Big Sweet against her arch rival, Ella Wall, a woman whose feats are also chronicled by Leadbelly and other country blues singers. Ella Wall enters the camp "jook" (a combination dance hall, gaming parlor and bawdy house) and sends a bold message to Big Sweet's man. The two women exchange verbal insults and then physical threats, until the conflict is halted by the arrival of the white quarters boss. While Ella Wall is disarmed and thrown off the job, Big Sweet stands up to the white man and refuses to yield her weapon. Her erstwhile lover expresses the admiration of the group in a telling compliment: "You wuz noble! You wuz uh whole woman and half uh man."[16] Big Sweet's increased respect is not earned at the cost of her femininity. Her value as a woman is in fact enhanced by her fierce conduct. After the argument, her lover proudly escorts her home.

Zora Hurston knew that approval of Big Sweet was not shared by the world outside the lumber camp. The life of this hard-living, knife-toting woman was the stuff of myriad stereotypes. And Hurston seemed all too aware of this judgment when she wrote, "I thought of all I had to live for and turned cold at the thought of dying in a violent manner in a sordid sawmill camp." A dramatic revelation follows: "But for my very life I knew I couldn't leave Big Sweet if the fight came. She had been too faithful to me."[17] Hurston vows to stand by her friend. Passages such as this have caused some critics to accuse Hurston of being condescending and self-serving in her presentation of the poor. She does seem to be playing to her audience here; *sordid* voices their opinion of the camp and its people. It does not express Hurston's view. Her problem was to legitimize Big Sweet's conduct without defending it or positing sociological explanations for it. Her solution was to identify the sources of its legitimacy within the folk culture itself. Characteristically, her approach was subtle and easily overlooked by the casual reader; it was deliberate nonetheless. Just before the fight scene, Hurston described the visit of a traveling preacher to the camp. His sermon, "Behold de Rib," is a variant of the creation myth; its text is Genesis 2:21, its subject is female equality.

"Behold de Rib" is one of the book's highlights. It captures the pithy logic of folk wisdom, the rhythmic cadence and vivid imagery of the downhome preacher, and a good measure of folk humor. The preacher begins by defining his terms: he instructs his congregants, "Behold means to look and see," and invites them to "look at dis woman God done made." Before focusing on woman, however, he pauses to consider God's previous handiwork and envisions the acts of creation. A cluster of visual images along with the repetition of the phrase "I can see" unify this section of the sermon/poem, as the preacher bears witness to what can be seen through the "eye of Faith." God emerges as regent and warrior, striding through space, wearing the elements as a helmet, blowing storms through his lips. To make a place for the world, he seizes "de mighty axe of his proving power" and opens a gash in "stubborn-standing space." To light the heavens, "... God shook his head / And a thousand million diamonds / Flew out from his glittering crown / And studded de evening sky and made de stars."

This last is a familiar trope in black preaching and brings to mind James Weldon Johnson's poem, "The Creation." One notes that both speakers have an anthropomorphic conception of God, but in "The Creation" He is "lonely"; in his most stirring analogy the speaker compares Him to a "mammy" bending over her baby. A masculine, even martial, God presides over the world of sexual equality. Johnson's speaker ends his story before getting to what is the central event of "Behold de Rib." Here stars are lit especially to shine on sleeping man and emerging woman:

> So God put Adam into a deep sleep
> And took out a bone, ah hah!
> And it is said that it was a rib.
> Behold de rib!
> A bone out of a man's side.
> He put de man to sleep and made wo-man,
> And men and women been sleeping together ever since.
> Behold de rib!
> Brothers, if God
> Had taken dat bone out of man's head
> He would have meant for woman to rule, hah

If he had taken a bone out of his foot,
He would have meant for us to dominize and rule.
He could have made her out of back-bone
And then she would have been behind us.
But, no, God Almighty, he took de bone out of his side
So dat places de woman beside us;
Hah! God knowed his own mind.
Behold de rib!

The preacher has modulated to a comic key, deepening the humor by alluding to that most famous of folk sermons, "Dry Bones." Still, his message is a serious one, as is apparent in the conclusion when he calls on his listeners, male and female, to march to glory side by side "in step wid de host dat John saw."[18]

Its rhythm and imagery place "Behold de Rib" squarely in the tradition of black preaching, but its message is anomalous. Female equality was not, is not, a common subject in black sermons. Hurston had transcribed other sermons in her field notes, including the one that became the centerpiece of her first novel, *Jonah's Gourd Vine*. Her selection of "Behold de Rib" was deliberate and so was its placement in *Mules and Men*. It prepares the reader to accept and approve Big Sweet's actions in the conflict that follows. She is heroic, as any man who similarly defended his honor would be. Although Hurston draws no connection between the sermon and the struggle—here and throughout the book her method is presentational, not analytical—the reader's approbation of Big Sweet is won in part by the juxtaposition of the two scenes.

The portrayal of Big Sweet anticipates the process of self-discovery Hurston's fictional heroines undergo. Like her, they must learn to manipulate language. The novels disclose Hurston's awareness that women, like children, are encouraged to be seen but not heard. She knew that few women had joined the lying sessions on Joe Clark's store porch in Eatonville; Big Sweet was one of a small number of female storytellers in the folklore collection. It was Big Sweet's talk though that first captured Hurston's attention. Her words were emblematic of her power, for they signaled her ownership of self. The ability to back up words with actions was a second indicator of an independent self. The care Hurston took to legitimize Big Sweet's behavior intimated the expected reactions to an assertive woman. Nevertheless, Hurston believed that individual black women could base their personal autonomy on communal traditions. In so doing, her characters achieved their status as heroines.

Lucy Potts Pearson is such a character. Although her husband John is its main protagonist, *Jonah's Gourd Vine* traces Lucy's coming of age as well as his. Loosely based on the lives of Hurston's parents, *Jonah's Gourd Vine* tells the story of Lucy and John's courtship and marriage, John's swift rise to prominence as a Baptist preacher, his equally swift fall resulting from his marital infidelities, Lucy's strength and perseverance, and the family's ultimate dissolution. All this takes place against a background of social and technological change occurring in the South around the turn of the century. These changes are subordinate to the cultural traditions that remain intact: the sermons and sayings, children's games and rhymes, hoodoo beliefs and practices. In the foreground are the experiences of John and Lucy. Lucy dies two thirds of the way through the novel, but her spirit hovers above it until the end.

That talk, and especially women's talk, as a major concern of the book is established on the very first page. Ned Crittenden accuses his wife, John's mother, of "always talkin' more'n yuh know."[19] Amy Crittenden is undaunted, "Ah changes jes ez many words ez Ah durn please!", but her ability to act on her words is limited. An ex-slave whose eldest son John is the child of her former master, Amy has been "freed" to a marriage with a ne'er-do-well sharecropper. Abused by a husband who is unable to "treasure" his children as she does, Amy must watch him hire John out to a white man, the equivalent of selling him into slavery. Amy's resistance is covert: she encourages her son to escape his stepfather's tyranny by seeking work on the plantation owned by his unacknowledged white father. John's return to the town of his birth adheres to the pattern of the young man arriving from the provinces. Every new thing, from shoes to trains, is a source of fascination. But the greatest fascination is with words. The verbal play of the plantation's children, the ribald ditties of youths, and the prayers and sermons of the elders spark John's imagination. To win Lucy's love, he must learn to speak for himself. Both lovers search for words that can express mutual affection and respect.

Their effort is complicated by class distinctions within the community. John is an "over-the-creek nigger" with no prospects.

Lucy's father is a land-owner, and her mother has arranged for her to marry a well-to-do farmer when she is of age. John has no education. Lucy is the star pupil in her school, famed for the long recitations she commits to memory. Though attracted to Lucy from the first, John finds her difficult to approach:

> When the opportunity presented itself he couldn't find words. Handling Big 'Oman, Lacey, Semmie, Bootsie and Mehaley merely called for action, but with Lucy he needed words and words that he did not have.

Recognizing that Lucy will not be swayed by the charms that capture other girls' affection, John yearns to master her language. Lucy assures him that he can learn recitations better than she, and he enrolls in school. Neither realizes that the needed words cannot be found in textbooks. They can only be learned from a deeper engagement with the folk culture. John achieves this when he spends a time in a work camp, where "next to showing muscle-power, [he] loved to tell stories." Upon his return, he is prepared to court Lucy in the traditional style. This time she is the one who must master a new tongue.

Robert Hemenway has identified the folkloric origins of the courtship ritual John employs.[20] Organized around the riddle—"are you a flying lark or a setting dove?"—the ritual allows the questioner to ascertain a woman's availability and willingness to pursue romance. A problem arises in the novel because the woman-child Lucy (she is only fourteen) does not know how to respond to the question. She had begun the conversation gaily, coyly matching wits with John. But as John broached more substantive concerns, "Lucy suddenly lost her fluency of speech." John presses this point thus:

> "Lucy, you pay much 'tention tuh birds?"
> "Unhunh. De Jay bird say 'Laz'ness will kill you,' and he go to hell Friday and totes uh grain uh sand in his mouf tuh put out de fire, and doves say, 'Where you *been* so long?'"
> John cut her short. "Ah I don't mean dat way, Lucy. Whut Ah wants tuh know is, which would you ruther be, if you had yo' ruthers—uh lark uh flyin', uh uh dove uh settin'?"
> "Ah don't know whut you talkin' 'bout, John. It mus' be uh new riddle."

"Naw 'tain't, Lucy. Po' me, Lucy. Ahm uh one wingded bird. Don't leave me lak dat, Lucy."

Far from new, the riddle is ancient and is meant to elicit a formulaic response. If Lucy wants to encourage John's advances, she should identify herself as a flying lark. Her ignorance of the proper answer imperils the future of the relationship. Lucy is resourceful enough to sift through her memory for plausible replies. She does not hit upon the correct one, but she does keep the conversation going. Her references to the jaybird, for example, demonstrates her awareness that the answer is to be found in folk traditions. The reference is to a familiar folktale, a variant of which, interestingly, is recounted by Big Sweet in *Mules and Men*. Here it is beside the point, as John's quick rejoinder makes clear. He poses the riddle directly. Lucy's continued inability to respond calls forth a plaintive cry: "Po' me, Lucy. Ahm uh one wingded bird."

Although her book learning is commendable, Lucy is clearly not sufficiently conversant with the rituals of her own culture. This suggests an immaturity and lack of experience that would render her an unsuitable wife. The situation is saved only when Lucy helps John improvise a new ritual that can substitute for the old. The instrument is a handkerchief out of which John has crafted what Hurston calls "a love knot." The lovers hold opposite ends of it throughout the conversation, and when Lucy misses the riddle, she points John's attention to the knot. Regaining her ground, she asks John to state what is on his mind. Wary, he asks first for a kiss ("Kiss me and loose me so Ah kin talk.") The kiss unlocks the poetic power that characterizes John's speech for the rest of the novel:

> "Lucy, Ah looked up intuh Heben and Ah seen you among de angels right 'round de throne, and when Ah seen *you*, mah heart swole up and put wings on mah shoulders, and Ah 'gin tuh fly 'round too, but Ah never would uh knowed yo' name if ole Gab'ull hadn't uh whispered it tuh me."

Lucy has reconferred John's wings. Though not as thoroughly grounded in the folk culture as he, she is knowledgeable enough to induce him to state his proposal in terms they *both* can understand. When he does, she accepts.[21] Their acting out of the courtship ritual predicts a marriage between two active partners, both of whom are able to manipulate language and negotiate respect between themselves and with others. It does not, however, foretell a marriage between equals. The prerogatives of maleness ultimately undo the balance.

Although he continues to profess and feel love and respect for Lucy, John Pearson does not remain faithful to her. His philandering, which begins shortly after the marriage and continues until her death, not only causes her great emotional pain but frequently jeopardizes the well-being of the entire family. He struggles against his weakness, expresses remorse when he fails, yet lacks all insight into his behavior. A serious flaw in the novel is Hurston's failure to provide a compelling motivation for John's conduct. A reader may infer that John's irresponsibility is, at least in part, a legacy of slavery. The plantation owner's initial reaction to John is, "What a fine stud." He projects all of his sexual fantasies on to John, labelling him at one point "a walking orgasm. A living exultation." John's sexual misadventures never cease to enthrall this man, who aids him in escaping rather than standing up to their consequences. In a period of transition between slavery and freedom, John remains bound by the slaveholder's conception of black men.

Lucy is, by contrast, a new black woman. Whenever John is irresponsible, Lucy is prepared to compensate. What he lacks in ambition and initiative, she is more than able to supply. She had defied her family to marry him and remains steadfast in her love and loyalty. She even looks with compassion on John's struggle to conquer the "brute beast" within, a struggle that intensifies after he is called to the ministry. John's spiritual call is genuine, but his acceptance of it also permits him to design a self-image independent of the white world. His move to Eatonville has further encouraged this possibility. There he can assume his rightful role as leader, his talents can be given free rein. The canker that galls is his recognition that Lucy deserves much of the credit for his success.

John's fellows are not blind to this fact, and they enjoy baiting him with the knowledge: "Aw, 'tain't you, Pearson, ... iss dat li'l' handful uh woman you got on de place." His resentment of his dependence on Lucy grows and expresses itself in his demand for her total dependence on him. A comparison of the following passage with the courtship ritual discussed above measures the damage the marriage suffers.

> "Lucy, is you sorry you married me instid uh some big nigger wid uh whole heap uh money and titles hung on tuh him?"
> "Whut make you ast me dat? If you tired uh me, jus' leave, me. Another man over de fence waiting fuh yo' job."

John's reaction to Lucy's verbal play is a violent threat; he will kill her if she ever repeats that fanciful remark. He stakes out claims of ownership, vowing to be Lucy's first and last man. Calming himself, he asks why Lucy has said such a thing. Her response is telling: "Aw, John, you know dat's jus' uh by-word. Ah hears all de women say dat." Lucy is answering John in terms sanctioned by the folk culture, terms that allow for her autonomy. She is engaging in the same kind of verbal sparring the courtship ritual required. The "by-word" would permit Lucy to negotiate respect in this exchange too, but John is no longer concerned with Lucy's ability to participate in cultural traditions. He concedes that the expression is a common one, but forbids her to use it.

Lucy continues to be supportive of John's career. Through her maneuvering, John becomes pastor of a large church, moderator of the State Baptist Association, and mayor of Eatonville. He can never accept her assistance as a complement to his gifts. He accuses: "You always tryin' tuh tell me whut tuh do. Ah wouldn't be where Ah is, if Ah didn't know more'n you think Ah do. You ain't mah guardzeen nohow." John's real defense against what he perceives to be Lucy's domination is other women. Of course, she cannot retaliate in kind. Words are her only defense, righteous, chastising words that strike fear in John's heart but fail to make him change his ways.

The climactic exchange takes one back to the opening pages of the novel. In his home, though not outside it, John has come to resemble Ned Crittenden, telling his wife to shut her mouth. Like Amy, Lucy refuses to be silenced. Instead she reproaches John severely and claims rights for herself and her children. "Big talk, she tells him, 'ain't changin' whut you doin'. You can't clean yo' self wid yo' tongue lak uh cat." For the first time in their marriage, John strikes his wife. This action, Hurston later suggested, prompted the novel's title. Taken from Jonah

4:6–10, the title refers to the gourd vine which grew profusely and gave the prophet shade. The next morning a worm attacked the vine and it withered. Thus did God punish his disobedient servant. To Hurston the Biblical story represented: "Great and sudden growth. One act of malice and it is withered and gone."[22] Slapping Lucy marks the beginning of the end for John; his public fortunes decline, and his private life falls into disarray. Years later he has no understanding of what has happened to him. It is literally the end for Lucy, who dies of an illness soon after. Unlike John, however, she has learned something from her experiences, a lesson she passes on to her favorite daughter. "Don't you love nobody better'n you do yo'self. Do, you'll be dying befo' yo' time is out."

Though Lucy's insight is personal, she has expressed it in the manner of a folk proverb. Throughout the novel, her speech is aphoristic. Sayings like the still current "God sho' don't like ugly" and the less familiar, more ingenious "God don't eat okra" (in other words, He doesn't like crooked, slick ways) roll easily off Lucy's tongue. She has mastered the language and absorbed much of the wisdom of her culture. In the end, she apprehends some of its limitations. She hears the silence where the sayings affirming female identity should be. She espies the untaught knowledge that no one can live through someone else and begins to teach it. Without her realizing it, the folk culture through her husband had assigned Lucy Pearson a "place"; she warns her daughter to be on guard against such a fate. Loving John too much, she has acquiesced in her own suppression. At her death, she remains on the threshold of self-discovery.

Although Lucy is the character who is given insight, the novel is less hers than John's. He becomes the central character because he serves the author's purposes beyond the demands of the plot. A contemporary reviewer rightly called *Jonah's Gourd Vine* a "talkfest," and a recent critic describes it as "a series of linguistic moments." Both discern that language is Hurston's priority. Published before *Mules and Men* though written afterward, the novel was Hurston's first opportunity to share at length the discoveries of her fieldwork. She incorporated so much of her research that one reviewer objected to her characters being mere pegs on which she hung their dialect and folkways.[23] The objection is grossly overstated, but it does highlight a problem in the book. Too often the folklore overwhelms the formal narrative. The novel is enriched nonetheless by its numerous examples of the Negro's "will to adorn," many of the expressions coming directly from Hurston's notes. She believed resolutely that blacks aspired for and achieved beauty in their verbal expression. With extraordinary care, she sought to reproduce their speech exactly as it was spoken. Given these concerns, John Pearson's was necessarily the key role. As preacher, hence poet, he represented the verbal artistry of his people at its height. He became, in the words of critic Larry Neal, "the intelligence of the community, the bearer of its traditions and highest possibilities."[24] This profound engagement with his culture causes John's struggle to reconcile his physical and spiritual selves to take precedence over Lucy's effort to claim her autonomy. In Hurston's second and most compelling novel, the female quest is paramount. The heroine, through acquiring an intimate knowledge of the folk culture, gains the self-knowledge necessary for true fulfillment.

With the publication of *Their Eyes Were Watching God*, it was clear that Zora Neale Hurston was an artist in full command of her talent. Here the folk material complements rather than overwhelms the narrative. The sustained beauty of Hurston's prose owes much to the body of folk expression she had recorded and studied, but much to the body of maturity of her individual voice. The language of this novel *sings*. Unlike Lucy, Janie, the heroine of *Their Eyes*, is a fully realized character. During the twenty-odd years spanned by the plot, she grows from a diffident teenager to a woman in complete possession of her self. Two recurring metaphors, the pear tree and the horizon, help unify the narrative. The first symbolizes organic union with another, the second, the individual experiences one must acquire to achieve selfhood. Early reviewers thought of the novel as a love story, but recent commentators designate Janie's search for identity as the novel's major theme. Following the pattern we have observed, Janie's self-discovery depends on her learning to manipulate language. Her success is announced in the novel's prologue when, as a friend listens in rapt attention, Janie begins to tell her own story.

The action of the novel proper begins when Janie is sixteen, beautiful, and eager to struggle with life, but unable to articulate her wishes and dreams. Her consciousness awakens as she watches bees fertilizing the blossoms of a pear tree. In the following passage, the narrative voice is not Janie's but the scene, like the novel as a whole, expresses her point of view:

She was stretched on her back beneath the pear tree soaking in the alto chant of the visiting bees, the gold of the sun and the planting breath of the breeze when the inaudible voice of it all came to her. She saw a dust-bearing bee sink into the sanctum of a bloom; the thousand sister-calyxes arch to meet the love embrace and the ecstatic shiver of the tree from root to tiniest branch creaming in every blossom and frothing with delight. So this was a marriage! She had felt a pain remorseless sweet that left her limp and languid.[25]

The lyricism of the passage mutes somewhat its intensely sexual imagery. Still, the image is remarkably explicit for a woman novelist of Hurston's time. Janie's response to the scene and her acceptance of its implications for her own life are instructive: "Oh to be a pear tree—*any* tree in bloom!" Janie acknowledges sexuality as a natural part of life, a major aspect of her identity. Before she has the chance to act on this belief, however, her grandmother interposes a radically different viewpoint.

To Nanny, her granddaughter's nascent sexuality is alarming. Having been unable to protect herself and her daughter from sexual exploitation, Nanny determines to safeguard Janie. Janie must repress her sexuality in order to avoid sexual abuse; the only haven is marriage. Marriage had not been an option for nanny, who as a slave was impregnated by her master; her mistress had forced her to flee with her newborn infant. Her daughter was raped by a black schoolteacher, convincing Nanny that male treachery knows no racial bounds. The world has thwarted her dreams of what a woman should be for herself and her daughter, "Ah wanted to preach a great sermon about colored women sittin' on high, but they wasn't no pulpit for me," but she has saved the text for Janie. She envisions her on the pedestal reserved for southern white women, far above the drudgery that has characterized Nanny's own life—the drudgery that has made the black woman "de mule uh de world." She arranges for Janie to marry Logan Killicks, an old man whose sixty acres and a mule constitute his eligibility. "The vision of Logan Killicks was desecrating the pear tree, but Janie didn't know how to tell Nanny that." So she assents to her grandmother's wish.

Joe Starks offers Janie an escape from her loveless marriage. He arrives just after Logan Killicks, despairing of his efforts to win his wife's affection by "pampering" her, has bought a second mule and ordered

Janie to plow alongside him. Perceiving that Killicks's command threatens to reduce her to the status her grandmother abhorred, Janie decides to escape with Joe. Their marriage fulfills Nanny's dreams. Eventually it causes Janie to understand that the old woman's dreams are not her own. Initially though, Joe Starks cuts a fine figure. Stylishly dressed and citified, he is a man of great ambition and drive. He is like no *black* man Janie has ever seen. He reminds her vaguely of successful white men, but she cannot grasp the implications of the resemblance. She can appreciate his big plans and the élan with which he courts her. Tempering her reservations that "he did not represent sun-up and pollen and blooming trees," Janie resolves, "he spoke for far horizon. He spoke for change and chance."

It quickly becomes apparent that, like Nanny, Joe has borrowed his criteria for success from the white world. He takes Janie to Eatonville because there, he believes, he can be a "big ruler of things." His ambition is soon realized. He buys property and opens a store which becomes the town's meeting place. He decrees that roads be dug, a post office established, a street lamp installed, and town incorporation papers drawn. Already landlord, storekeeper, and postmaster, Joe runs for mayor to consolidate his power. After his election, he builds a large white house that is a travesty of a plantation mansion, and then furnishes it in the grand manner right down to brass spittoons. His brashness elicits equal measures of respect and resentment from the townspeople. As much as they admire his accomplishments, they take exception to his manner. One citizen's observation is widely shared: "he loves obedience out of everybody under de sound of his voice."

Everybody naturally includes Janie. Joe assigns her the role of "Mrs. Mayor Starks." She must hold herself apart from the townspeople, conduct herself according to the requirements of his position. Under no circumstances must she speak in public. Starks first imposes this rule during a ceremony marking the opening of the store. The ceremony has occasioned much speechmaking, and toward the end, Janie is invited to say a few words. Before she can respond, her husband takes the floor to announce:

> Thank yuh fuh yo' compliments, but mah wife don't know nothin' 'bout no speech-makin'. Ah never married her for nothin' lak dat. She's uh woman and her place is in de home.

Joe's announcement takes Janie by surprise. Unsure that she even wants to speak, she strongly resents being denied the right to decide for herself. Joe's prohibitions increase. He forbids Janie to participate in the lying sessions held on the store porch; she is hustled inside when they begin. Janie loves these conversations and notes that Joe, while not deigning to join in, stays around to listen and laugh. Being forbidden to speak is a severe penalty in an oral culture. It short-circuits Janie's attempt to claim an identity of her own, robs her of the opportunity to negotiate respect from her peers. Barred from speaking to anyone but Joe, she loses the design to say anything at all. "So gradually, she pressed her teeth together and learned to hush."

After seven years of marriage, Janie recognizes that Joe requires her total submission. She yields. As she does so however, she retains a clear perception of herself and her situation, a perception that becomes her salvation in the end. On one occasion after Joe has slapped her (for naturally, her submission has not slowed his verbal or physical abuse) she experienced the following revelation:

> Janie stood where he left her for unmeasured time and thought. She stood here until something fell off the shelf inside her. Then she went inside to see what it was. It was her image of Jody tumbled down and shattered. But looking at it she saw that it never was the flesh and blood figure of her dreams. Just something she had grabbed up to drape her dreams over. In a way she turned her back upon the image where it lay and looked further. She had no more blossomy openings dusting pollen over her man, neither any glistening young fruit where the petals used to be. She found that she had a host of thoughts she had never expressed to him, and numerous emotions she had never let Jody know about. Things packed up and put away in parts of her heart where he could never find them. She was saving up feelings for some man she had never seen. She had an inside and an outside now and suddenly she knew how not to mix them.

Facing the truth about Joe allows Janie to divorce him emotionally. She accepts her share of responsibility for the failure of the marriage, knowing now that if Joe has used her for his purposes, she has used him for hers. Yet she understands that her dreams have not impinged on Joe's selfhood; they have been naive but not destructive. By creating inside and outside selves, she hopes to insulate the core of her being from the destructive consequences of Joe's dreams. She cannot claim her autonomy, because she is not yet capable of imagining herself except in relationship to a man. Still, she is no longer willing to jeopardize her inner being for the sake of any such relationship.

Janie remains content to practice a kind of passive resistance against Joe's tyranny until he pushes her to the point when she must "talk smart" to salvage her self-respect. For many years, Joe has forced her to clerk in the store, taking every opportunity to ridicule her for minor mistakes. As he grows older, he adds taunts about her age to his repertoire of verbal insults. Sensing that her womanhood as well as her intelligence is under attack, she retaliates: "Humph! Talkin' 'bout *me* lookin' old! When you pull down yo' britches, you look lak de change uh life." So unaccustomed is Joe to hearing his wife "specify" that he imputes nefarious motives to her words. Ill and suspicious, he hires a hoodoo doctor to counteract the curse he believes Janie is putting on him. No curse exists, of course, but Starks is dying of kidney disease and of mortal wounds to his vanity. As he lies on his deathbed, Janie confronts him with more painful truths. Again she reveals how well she comprehends the effect of his domination: "Mah own mind had tuh be squeezed and crowded out tuh make room for yours in me."

The attack on her dying husband is not an act of gratuitous cruelty; it is an essential step toward self-reclamation. Moreover, in terms of the narrative, the deathbed episode posits a dramatic break with Janie's past. She is henceforth a different woman. Independent for the first time in her life, she exults in the "freedom feeling." Reflecting on her past, she realizes that her grandmother, though acting out of love, has wronged her deeply. At base, Nanny's sermon had been about things, when Janie wanted to journey to the horizons in search of people. Janie is able at last to reject her grandmother's way and resume her original quest. That quest culminates in her marriage to Tea Cake Woods with whom she builds a relationship totally unlike the others she has had.

Tea Cake is a troubadour, a traveling bluesman, whose life is dedicated to joyful pursuits. With this character, Hurston explores an alternative definition of manhood, one that does not rely on external manifestations of power, money, and position. Tea Cake has none of these. He is so thoroughly immune to the influence of white American society that he does not even desire them. Tea Cake is at ease being who and what he is. Consequently, he fosters the growth of Janie's self-acceptance. Together they achieve the ideal sought by most characters in Hurston's fiction. They trust emotion over intellect, value the spiritual over the material, preserve a sense of humor and are comfortable with their sensuality. Tea Cake confirms Janie's right to self-expression and invites her to share equally in their adventures. She sees that he "could be a bee to a blossom—a pear tree blossom in the spring." Over the protests of her neighbors, she marries this man several years younger than she whose only worldly expression is a guitar.

They embark on a nomadic existence which takes them to the rich farmland of the Florida Everglades where both Tea Cake and Janie work on the muck and where both share household chores. Their cabin becomes "the unauthorized center of the job," the focal point of the community like the store in Eatonville. Here, however, Janie "could listen and laugh and even talk some herself if she wanted to. She got so she could tell big stories herself from listening to the rest." This is an important and hard-won accomplishment. Even Tea Cake, strongly idealized character though he is, has had difficulty accepting Janie's full participation in their life together. Zora Hurston knew that Tea Cake, a son of the folk culture, would have inherited its negative attitudes toward women. She knew besides that female autonomy cannot be granted by men, it must be demanded by women. Janie gains her autonomy only when she insists upon it. Under pressure, Tea Cake occasionally falls back on the prerogatives of his sex. His one act of physical cruelty results from his need to show someone else who is boss in his home. In the main, though, Tea Cake transcends the chauvinistic attitudes of the group. He largely keeps his pledge to Janie that she "partake wid everything."

The marriage of Janie and Tea Cake ends in the wake of a fierce hurricane that is vividly evoked in the novel. In the process of saving Janie's life, Tea Cake is bitten by a rabid dog. Deranged, he tries to kill Janie, and she shoots him in self-defense. Despite these events, the conclusion of *Their Eyes Were Watching God* is not tragic. For, with Tea Cake as her guide, Jane has explored the soul of her culture and learned how to value herself. This fact is underscored in the prologue and epilogue of the novel, sections set after Janie's return to Eatonville following Tea Cake's death. In the former, she tells her friend Pheoby: "Ah been a delegate to de big 'ssociation of life. Yessuh! De Grand Lodge, de big convention of livin' is just where Ah been dis year and a half y'all ain't seen me." Having been to the horizon and back, as she puts it, she is eager to teach the crucial lesson she has learned in her travels. Everybody must do two things for themselves: "They got tuh go tuh God, and they got tuh find out about livin' fuh theyselves." This is Janie's text; the sermon she preaches is the novel itself. She has claimed the right to change her own words.

Hurston was never to duplicate the triumph of *Their Eyes Were Watching God*. In her subsequent novels, she changed the direction of her work dramatically. *Moses: Man of the Mountain* (1939) is a serio-comic novel which attempts to fuse Biblical narrative and folk myth. *Seraph on the Suwanee* (1948) is a psychological novel whose principal characters are upwardly mobile white Floridians. Although Hurston's willingness to experiment is admirable, the results are disappointing. Neither of her net settings is as compelling as the Eatonville milieu. Though the impact of black folk expression is always discernible, it is diminished and so is the power of Hurston's own voice. In these novels, the question of female autonomy recedes in importance, and when it is posed in *Seraph*, the answer is decidedly reactionary. What is of interest in terms of this essay is Hurston's reworking of themes identified in her earlier work.

Hurston's Moses is a combination of Biblical lawgiver and Afro-American hoodoo man. He is officially a highborn Egyptian, but according to legend, he is a Hebrew; Moses neither wholly rejects nor accepts the legend. The uncertainties about his identity complicate his question for fulfillment. That quest conforms in part to the pattern we have outlined. Moses becomes a great manipulator of language, and much of his authority derives from the power of his Words. As an educated man, he has been taught the formal language of the Egyptian elite. He later spends many years with the Midianites in spiritual preparation for his divinely appointed task; this period is somewhat comparable to John Pearson's stay in the work camp and Janie's sojourn on the muck. With the Midianites, Moses adapts to the rhythms of a rural folk culture and learns to speak more colloquial English. The Hebrews speak in the black folk idiom, and when he becomes their leader, Moses masters their tongue. Moses is of course a man of action, and as befits a leader, he fights most often for the rights of those under his stewardship. Though he knows he would be more beloved as a king and more popular as a politician, Moses rejects the accouterments of power. He has as little use for class distinctions as Janie and Tea Cake. In Moses, Hurston developed a character who was already a certified hero, not only in the Judeo-Christian tradition, but according to her introduction, also among the peoples of Asia and Africa. What she adds are new points of emphasis, and these had precedents in her earlier work. The most important is implicit in her attempt to reconcile the Biblical Moses and her conception of Moses as conjurer. Hurston had been the first scholar ever to research hoodoo in America and had studied the more systematic religion of Vodun in Haiti. In both instances, she had noted the coexistence of seemingly antithetical religious beliefs in the lives of her informants. In *Moses: Man of the Mountain*, one looks in vain for a synthesis of the two belief systems to which the hero is heir. Hurston simply allows them to coexist. In a novel whose protagonist seeks and achieves cosmic fulfillment, the failure to explicate the spiritual sources of that fulfillment is serious indeed.

Moses is a very ambitious novel. If it fails in some respects, it succeeds in others. It offers a very effective satire on the transition from slavery to freedom for black Americans. Hurston drew on the long-standing identification of blacks with the enslaved Hebrews, the identification that had inspired the majestic spiritual "Go Down, Moses" and countless other sacred and secular expressions. Most dwelt on the sufferings of bondage and the joys of emancipation. Hurston's concerns were the responsibilities of freedom. In the novel, the people of Goshen are hesitant to rebel against slavery and unable to fully comprehend freedom. Hurston satirizes their ready assent to the commands of their slavemasters and their reluctance to follow Moses. She mocks the vainglory of self-appointed leaders and the failure of the people to understand the need for sacrifice. Their petty bickering and constant backbiting are also objects of her ridicule. Hurston's satirical sallies are invariably good-natured and often very funny. But her novel is not the serious statement about faith and freedom she seems to have intended.

Hurston did not publish another novel for nine years. In the interim, her political instincts grew markedly conservative. World War II and its Cold War aftermath hastened the rightward drift of her thinking. At the suggestion of her publisher, she revised the manuscript of *Dust Tracks on a Road* to eliminate sections critical of the American system; as it was published in 1942, her autobiography seemed a celebration of the American way. Through the decade, Hurston contributed a number of articles to the *American Mercury* and the *Saturday Evening Post* which developed patriotic themes. By the 1950s, her work was welcome in the pages of the *American Legion Magazine*. Not all of Hurston's articles were reactionary. Some applauded the achievements of blacks in various endeavors. Others reaffirmed her belief in the value of black folklore, though she had ceased her research in the field. A few pieces, written for *Negro Digest*, protested racism in diplomacy, publishing, and everyday life. On the whole, however, Hurston's political views, which she expounded more often in the 1940s than at any other time in her life, supported the status quo. The same charge might be leveled at her last work of fiction, *Seraph on the Suwanee*.

This novel restates the major themes of *Their Eyes Were Watching God*, perhaps in a misguided attempt to universalize them. Here the protagonist is Arvay Henson Meserve, who like Janie searches for self-identity. She is hindered in her quest by the deep-rooted inferiority she feels about her poor cracker background. For the wrong reason, she has come to the right conclusion. As Hurston depicts her, she is inferior to her husband Jim and the only identity she can attain is through accepting her subordinate role as his wife. Hurston endows Jim Meserve with a mixture of the attractive qualities found in Joe Starks and Tea Cake. He is more crudely chauvinistic than either of them, but this aspect of his character is treated with amazing tolerance. Early in the novel, Arvay reflects that if she married Jim, "her whole duty as a wife was to just love him good, be nice and kind around the house and have children for him. She could do that and be more than happy and satisfied, but it looked too simple."[26] The novel demonstrates that it is much too simple, but at the conclusion the happiness Arvay supposedly realizes is achieved on exactly those terms. The problem is Hurston's inability to grant her protagonist the resources that would permit her to claim autonomy. Although Arvay "mounts the pulpit" at the end of the novel, she has no words of her own to speak.

Ultimately, Arvay's weakness may be less a personal problem than a cultural one. Though black characters play minor roles in the novel, black cultural traditions permeate the narrative. They influence everyone's speech, so much so that at times the whites sound suspiciously like the storytellers in Eatonville. Jim relishes the company of his black employees, whom he treats in a disgustingly condescending manner; and one of his sons, after being tutored by a black neighbor, leaves home to join a jazz band. Unlike the earlier protagonists, Arvay cannot attain her identity through a profound engagement with the folk culture, because she has no culture to engage. The culture of the people Arvay despises has supplanted her own. Seen from this perspective, *Seraph on the Suwanee* is not as anomalous or as reactionary as it otherwise, appears.

From any vantage point, however, it represents an artistic decline. Hurston was at her best when she drew her material directly from black folk culture; it was the source of her creative power. Throughout her career, she endeavored to negotiate respect for it, talking smart then sweet in her folklore and fiction, proclaiming its richness and complexity to all who would hear. Her most memorable characters are born of this tradition. In portraying them, she was always cognizant of the difficulties in reconciling the demands of community and the requirements of self, difficulties that were especially intense for women. The tension could not be resolved by rejecting the community or negating the self. Hurston challenged black people to dig deep into their culture to unearth the values on which it was built. Those values could restore the balance. They could give men and women words to speak. They could set their spirits free.

Notes

1. Introduction to *Their Eyes Were Watching God* (Urbana: University of Illinois Press, 1978), p. xiv.

2. *I Love Myself When I Am Laughing ... and Then Again When I Am Looking Mean and Impressive, A Zora Hurston Reader* (Old Westbury, N.Y.: The Feminist Press, 1979); the quotation is from Walker's introduction to Robert Hemenway, *Zora Neale Hurston: A Literary Biography* (Urbana: University of Illinois Press, 1977), p. xii.

3. "Between Laughter and Tears," review of *Their Eyes Were Watching God*, *New Masses* 23 (5 October 1937): 25.

4. June Jordan, "On Richard Wright and Zora Neale Hurston: Notes toward a Balancing of Love and Hatred," *Black World* (August 1974): 5.

5. "Characteristics of Negro Expression," [1934]; in *Voices from the Harlem Renaissance* ed. Nathan Huggins (New York: Oxford University Press, 1976), pp. 224–27. The expression "changing words" appears in several of Hurston's works. I suspect it derives from a form of the word "exchange," in which the weakly stressed syllable has been dropped. J. L. Dillard identifies the dropping of such syllables as a common characteristic of Black English. See *Black English* (New York: Random House, 1972), p. 249.

6. *I Love Myself*, p. 153.

7. Hemenway, *Zora Neale Hurston*, p. 62.

8. *Mules and Men* (1936; reprint ed., Bloomington: Indiana University Press, 1978), p. 3.

9. Quoted in Robert Hemenway, "Are You a Flying Lark or a Setting Dove," *Afro-American Literature: The Reconstruction of Instruction* (New York: Modern Language Association, 1979), p. 132.

10. Hemenway, *Zora Neale Hurston*, p. 168.

11. *Dust Tracks on a Road* (Philadelphia: J. B. Lippincott, 1942; rpt. 1971), pp. 186–91.

12. *Journal of American Folklore* 88 (Jan.–March 1975): 58.

13. Hurston first noted "this scornful attitude towards black women" in "Characteristics of Negro Expression," p. 234. For examples of sexism in folktales, see Daryl C. Dance, *Shuckin' and Jivin': Folklore from Black Americans* (Bloomington: Indiana University Press, 1978), pp. 110–42.

14. *Mules and Men*, p. 134.

15. Abrahams, "Negotiating Respect," pp. 58–62.

16. *Mules and Men*, p. 162.

17. *Mules and Men*, p. 160.

18. *Mules and Men*, pp. 148–51.

19. *Jonah's Gourd Vine* (Philadelphia: J. B. Lippincott, 1934; rpt. 1971), p. 9. All further references to this work appear in the text.

20. Hemenway, "Flying Lark or Setting Dove," pp. 134–38.

21. See Hemenway, "Flying Lark or Setting Dove," pp. 139–47, for an extended gloss on this passage. The essay as a whole has influenced my reading of the novel.

22. Hemenway, *Zora Neale Hurston*, p. 192.

23. John Chamberlain, *New York Times*, 3 May 1934, p. 7; Hemenway, *Zora Neale Hurston*, p. 192; Andrew Burris, review of *Jonah's Gourd Vine*, *Crisis* 41 (1934): 166.

24. Introduction to *Jonah's Gourd Vine*, p. 7.
25. *Their Eyes*, p. 24.
26. *Seraph on the Suwanee* (New York: Scribner's, 1948), p. 33.

Chronology

1891	Born to carpenter, sharecropper, and Baptist preacher John Hurston and Lucy Potts Hurston, a former schoolteacher, on January 7.
1901	January 7—usually and perhaps falsely claimed this as her birth date—making her 10 years younger.
1904	Mother Lucy Hurston dies.
1917	Begins high school at Morgan Academy in Baltimore.
1918	Receives high school diploma in June.
1918–19	Attends Howard Prep School.
1919–1924	Attends Howard University; earns less than two years of credits. Receives an associate degree from Howard in 1920.
1921	Publishes her first story, "John Redding Goes to Sea," in a campus magazine.
1924	Publishes short story "Drenched in Light" in *Opportunity* in December.
1925	January, arrives in New York just as the Harlem Renaissance begins to crest. May, wins *Opportunity* contest with "Spunk" and her play *Color Struck*; publishes "Spunk."
1925–1927	Receives scholarship from Annie Nathan Meyer and attends Barnard College, studying anthropology.
1926	Begins fieldwork for Franz Boas, father of anthropology. January, publishes "John Redding Goes

to Sea" in *Opportunity*. July, organizes *Fire!* with
Langston Hughes and Wallace Thurman. August,
publishes "Muttsy" in *Opportunity*. September,
publishes "Possum or Pig" in *The Forum*. November,
publishes only issue of *Fire!*, featuring her story
"Sweat."

1927   May 17, marries Herbert Sheen. October, publishes
"Cudjo's Own Story of the Last African Slaver" in the
Journal of Negro History. December, signs contract
with Mrs. Mason.

1928   Receives her Bachelor of Arts degree from Barnard.
January, separates from Sheen. May, publishes "How
It Feels to Be Colored Me" in the *World Tomorrow*.

1930   Works on the play *Mule Bone* with Langston Hughes.

1931   Divorces Sheen. Writes for *Fast and Furious*.

1932   Writes and stages *The Great Day*.

1933   Stages *From Sun to Sun* (a version of *Great Day*) at
Rollins College. August, publishes "The Gilded Six-
Bits" in *Story*.

1934   Publishes seven essays in Nancy Cunard's anthology,
Negro.

1934   Goes to Bethune-Cookman College to establish a
school of dramatic arts. May, publishes *Jonah's Gourd
Vine*. November, *Singing Steel* (a version of *Great Day*)
performed in Chicago.

1935   Studies for a Ph.D. in anthropology at Columbia
University on a fellowship from the Rosenwald
Foundation. Works with Alan Lomax on a Library of
Congress folk-music recording expedition. August,
joins the WPA Federal Theatre Project as a dramatic
coach. October, *Mules and Men* published.

1936   Awarded a Guggenheim Fellowship to study West
Indian Obeah Voodoo practices. Researches in
Jamaica.

1937   Writes *Their Eyes Were Watching God* in seven weeks.
May, returns to Haiti on a renewed Guggenheim
grant. September, *Their Eyes Were Watching God*
published.

1938	Writes *Tell My Horse*; published the same year. April, joins the Federal Writers Project in Florida to work on *The Florida Negro*.
1939	Publishes "Now Take Noses" in *Cordially Yours*. June, receives an honorary Doctor of Letters degree from Morgan State College. Marries Albert Price III in Florida. Hired as a drama instructor by North Carolina College for Negroes, Durham. November, *Moses, Man of the Mountain* published.
1940	Files for divorce from Price.
1941	Writes *Dust Tracks on a Road*. Works as a story consultant at Paramount Pictures.
1942	November, *Dust Tracks on a Road* published.
1943	Awarded the Anisfield-Wolf Book Award in Race Relations for *Dust Tracks on a Road*. Receives Howard University's Distinguished Alumni Award.
1945	Writes *Mrs. Doctor*; it is rejected by Lippincott.
1947	Goes to British Honduras to research; writes *Seraph on the Suwanee*.
1948	Accused of molesting a ten-year-old boy and arrested (case dismissed 1949). October, *Seraph on the Suwanee* published.
1956	Receives an award for "education and human relations" at Bethune-Cookman College.
1959	Enters the St. Lucie County Welfare Home.
1960	January 28, dies in the St. Lucie County Welfare Home; buried in an unmarked grave in the segregated Garden of Heavenly Rest, Fort Pierce.
1973	Alice Walker discovers and marks Hurston's grave.
1975	Walker publishes "In Search of Zora Neale Hurston," in *Ms.* magazine, launching a Hurston revival.
1993	Fort Pierce builds the Zora Neale Hurston Branch Library.

Works by Zora Neale Hurston

Jonah's Gourd Vine, 1934.

Mules and Men, 1935.

Their Eyes Were Watching God, 1937.

Tell My Horse, 1938.

Moses Man of the Mountain, 1939.

Dust Tracks on a Road, 1942.

Seraph on the Suwanee, 1948.

The Sanctified Church: The Folklore Writings of Zora Neale Hurston, 1981.

Spunk: The Selected Short Stories of Zora Neale Hurston, 1985.

Works about Zora Neale Hurston

Anderson, Jervis. *This Was Harlem: A Cultural Portrait*. New York: Farrar, Straus & Giroux, 1982.

Awkward, Michael. *Inspiriting Influences*. New York: Columbia University Press, 1989.

————, ed. *New essays on Their Eyes Were Watching God*. Cambridge: Cambridge University Press, 1991.

Baker, Houston A., Jr. *Black Literature in America*. New York: McGraw-Hill, 1971.

Bloom, Harold, ed. *Zora Neale Hurston*. New York: Chelsea House, 1986.

————, ed. *Zora Neale Hurston's Their Eyes Were Watching God*. New York: Chelsea House, 1987.

Cunard, Nancy, ed. *Negro: An Anthology*. New York: Ungar, 1970.

Davis, Rose Parkman. *Zora Neale Hurston: An Annotated Bibliography and Reference Guide*. Westport, Conn: Greenwood Press, 1997.

Gates, Henry Louis, Jr. *Zora Neale Hurston: Critical Perspectives Past and Present*. New York: Amistad Press, 1993.

————. "Their Eyes Were Watching God: Hurston and the Speakerly Text." Gates, 154–203.

Hemenway, Robert E. "Zora Neale Hurston and the Eatonville Anthropology." *The Harlem Renaissance Remembered*. Ed. Arna Bontemps. New York: Dodd, Mead and Co, 1972.

————. *Zora Neale Hurston: A Literary Biography*. Urbana and Chicago: University of Illinois Press, 1977.

Holloway, Karla. *The Character of the Word: The Texts of Zora Neale Hurston*. Westport, Conn: Greenwood Press, 1987.

hooks, bell. "Zora Neale Hurston: A Subversive Reading." *Matatu* (1989): 5–23.

Howard, Lillie Pearle. *Zora Neale Hurston*. Boston: Twayne, 1980.

Johnson, Barbara. "Metaphor, Metonymy, and Voice in Their Eyes." *Black Literature and Literary Theory*. Ed. Henry Louis Gates Jr., 205–221. New York: Methuen, 1984.

———. "Thresholds of Difference: Structures of Address in Zora Neale Hurston." *Zora Neale Hurston: Critical Perspectives Past and Present*. Ed. Henry Louis Gates Jr., 130–140. New York: Amistad Press, 1993.

Jordan, June. "On Richard Wright and Zora Neale Hurston." *Black World* 23 no. 10 (August 1974): 4–8.

Lewis, David Levering. *When Harlem Was in Vogue*. New York; Vintage Press, 1982.

Lowe, John. "Hurston, Humor, and the Harlem Renaissance." *The Harlem Renaissance Re-Examined*. Eds. Victor A. Kramer and Robert A. Russ. 283–313. New York: AMS, 1987.

———. *Jump at the Sun: Zora Neale Hurston's Cosmic Comedy*. Urbana: University of Illinois Press, 1994.

Meisenhelder, Susan Edwards. *Hitting a Straight Lick With a Crooked Stick: Race and Gender in the Work of Zora Neale Hurston*. Tuscaloosa: University of Alabama Press, 1999.

Nathiri, N.Y, ed. *Zora Neale Hurston: A Woman And Her Community*. Orlando: Sentinel Communications Company, 1991.

Newson, Adele S. *Zora Neale Hurston: A Reference Guide*. Boston: G.K. Hall, 1987.

Plant, Deborah G. "Metaphors of Self, Language, and the Will-to-Power." *Every Tub Must Sit on Its Own Bottom*. Urbana and Chicago: University of Illinois Press, 1995.

Rampersad, Arnold. *The Life of Langston Hughes*, Vol. 1, *I, Too Sing America 1902–1941*. New York: Oxford University Press, 1986.

Smith, Barbara. "Sexual Politics and the Fiction of Zora Neale Hurston." *Radical Teacher* 8. (May 1978): 26–30.

Stepto, Robert B. *From Behind the Veil: A Study of Afro-American Narrative*. Urbana: University of Illinois Press, 1979.

Turner, Darwin T. *In a Minor Chord: Three Afro-American Writers and Their Search for Identity.* Carbondale: Southern Illinois University Press, 1971.

Walker, Alice, ed. *I Love Myself When I'm Laughing: A Zora Neale Hurston Reader.* New York: The Feminist Press, 1979.

———. "In Search of Zora Neale Hurston." *Ms.* (March 1975): 74–79, 85–89.

Wall, Cheryl A. "Zora Neale Hurston's Traveling Blues." *Women of the Harlem Renaissance.* Bloomington and Indianapolis: Indiana University Press, 1995.

———. "Zora Neale Hurston: Changing Her Own Words." Gates 76–97.

Washington, Mary Helen. "The Black Woman's Search for Identity." *Black World* 21, no. 10. (August 1972): 68–75.

WEBSITES

Perspectives in American Literature: Zora Neale Hurston
www.csustan.edu/english/reuben/pal/chap9/hurston.html

Voices from the Gaps: Zora Neale Hurston
voices.cla.umn.edu/authors/ZoraNealeHurston.html

Zora Neale Hurston
www.cas.usf.edu/anthropology/women/hurston/Zora.html

Zora Neale Hurston
i.am/zora

Zora Neale Hurston, American Author
www-hsc.usc.edu/~gallaher/hurston/hurston.html

Zora Neale Hurston Festival
www.zoranealehurston.cc/

Zora Neale Hurston/Richard Wright Foundation
www.hurston-wright.org/

Contributors

HAROLD BLOOM is Sterling Professor of the Humanities at Yale University and Henry W. and Albert A. Berg Professor of English at the New York University Graduate School. He is the author of over 20 books, including *Shelley's Mythmaking* (1959), *The Visionary Company* (1961), *Blake's Apocalypse* (1963), *Yeats* (1970), *A Map of Misreading* (1975), *Kabbalah and Criticism* (1975), *Agon: Toward a Theory of Revisionism* (1982), *The American Religion* (1992), *The Western Canon* (1994), and *Omens of Millennium: The Gnosis of Angels, Dreams, and Resurrection* (1996). *The Anxiety of Influence* (1973) sets forth Professor Bloom's provocative theory of the literary relationships between the great writers and their predecessors. His most recent books include *Shakespeare: The Invention of the Human* (1998), a 1998 National Book Award finalist, *How to Read and Why* (2000), and *Genius: A Mosaic of One Hundred Exemplary Creative Minds* (2002). In 1999, Professor Bloom received the prestigious American Academy of Arts and Letters Gold Medal for Criticism, and in 2002 he received the Catalonia International Prize.

NORMA JEAN LUTZ is a long-time professional writer who lives in Tulsa, Oklahoma. Aside from having written numerous short stories and articles, Norma Jean has contributed a number of biographies to the *BioCritiques* series.

AMY SICKELS is a freelance writer living in New York City. She has published short stories, essays, and book reviews in numerous journals, including *Fourth Genre*, *Kalliope*, and *Literary Review*. She has taught at

Pennsylvania State University and holds a B.A. from Ohio University and a Master of Fine Arts in Creative Writing from Pennsylvania State University.

ROBERT HEMENWAY has served as a Professor of English at the University of Kentucky and Dean of Arts and Sciences at the University of Oklahoma. He has been the Chancellor of the University of Kansas since 1995. His book *Zora Neale Hurston: A Literary Biography* was listed by the *New York Times* among its "Best Books of 1978."

CHERYL A. WALL is department Chair and Professor of English at Rutgers University. She is the author of *Women of the Harlem Rennaissance* (1995), and editor of *Changing our Own Words: Essays on Criticism, Theory, and Writing by Black Women* (1989).

INDEX